Vicki Howie writes stories, plays and songs for young children, based on her work with the age group in the local church. She is author of Barnabas' popular resource books Easy ways to Christmas plays, Easy ways to seasonal plays, Easy ways to Bible fun for the very young, Easy to say, easy to play *and its accompanying CD. She lives in Kent with her husband and two children.*

Text copyright © Vicki Howie 2004
Illustrations copyright © Kathy Hughes 2004
p. 5: Poster artwork copyright © Jane Taylor 2001
The author asserts the moral right
to be identified as the author of this work

Published by
The Bible Reading Fellowship
First Floor, Elsfield Hall
15–17 Elsfield Way, Oxford OX2 8FG

ISBN 1 84101 342 0
First published 2004
10 9 8 7 6 5 4 3 2 1 0

A catalogue record for this book is available from the
British Library

Printed and bound in Malta

Easy ways to SEASONAL FUN for the Very Young

Vicki Howie

Twelve Bible-based activities for 3–5s

CONTENTS

Friendly fun-filled meetings for parents or carers and pre-school children with Bible-based stories and activities

at

_____

_____

on

_____

between _____

Contact:

_____

Refreshments _____

Introduction

Easy ways to seasonal fun for the very young is a simple but comprehensive resource book for those working with the 3–5s both in church-based pre-school groups and in primary education. It provides the busy church leader or schoolteacher with twelve seasonal sessions that explore the major church festivals and highlight the changing seasons. In each session, the children have fun:

- listening to an everyday story about Teddy
- examining the objects in the story basket
- singing songs and listening to music
- miming or playing simple drama games
- learning about the natural world from the nature table
- completing a simple craft activity
- saying a prayer

These activities are especially designed to help the children understand the Bible story that follows. In addition, there are two mimed nativity plays, suggested celebrations for harvest, Easter and All Saints' Day, a summer picnic for your group and a summer pram service or toddler praise.

Only a small amount of preparation is required (outlined in the 'Ready… Steady… Go…' sections at the beginning of each session). Simply take the book to each meeting or lesson and work from it, using the headings as your cribsheet.

How the book works

You may like to have 'story time' at the same time of day or at the same time in each meeting. If parents or carers are present, this time could be when the adults have finished their coffee and the children want a break from playing. Put some of the toys away so that the children are not distracted by them. Encourage the children to sit around you on rugs, with the adults seated in a semicircle behind them. Don't worry if some children would prefer to sit on their parents' laps.

Welcome

Use the 'Welcome' section to remind yourself to give everyone a warm welcome to the group. (Don't let anyone come in and sit on their own.) Space has been left for you to write in the names of any newcomers or speaker, so that you can introduce them to your regular group. (You may like to sing the song 'You are welcome' from *Feeling Good!* published by Church House Publishing, a collection of simple songs written especially for younger children.)

For the adults

The paragraph headed 'For the adults' reminds you to tell the adults about the day's theme and helps you to explain the meaning of the Bible story they will hear being read to the children.

Notices

Fill in any notices in advance, in the space provided. Use this opportunity to tell everyone about a new baby, to publicize church or school events and to remind them of the next meeting or class.

Happy birthday

The children will thoroughly enjoy singing 'Happy birthday' to anyone with a birthday close to the day of the meeting. Find out their names during coffee time and write them down in the space provided. Singing the song is a good way to gain the children's attention, so be ready with Teddy and your story basket immediately afterwards.

Teddy and the story basket

You will find it much easier to entertain the children and hold their attention if you use a teddy (or other soft-toy character) each week to help you tell the simple story based on the objects you have brought in your story basket or story box (see below). You could give him the same name as your group (for example, Rainbow Teddy, First Steps Teddy, Sunbeam Teddy). The children will identify with Teddy as he learns all about God's wonderful world and asks the questions that they may be too shy to ask. If you are at all shy yourself about being in the limelight, you will find that Teddy will draw everyone's attention away from you—their eyes will be on him.

Make Teddy as lovable, mischievous and comical as you can—rather like a small child. Practise with him at home, making him jump up and down, wave at the children, look in the basket and whisper in your ear. (If you have any doll's clothes or baby clothes of the right size, dress him in different clothes each time to suit your theme.)

You may like to bring along additional teddies to play the parts of Mr and Mrs Bear and Little Ted (Teddy's baby brother), who are mentioned in some of the stories.

The story basket

Find an intriguing story basket or box (with a lid) in which to bring the objects suggested in the 'Ready' section. A traditional picnic hamper basket is ideal because you can keep the buckles done up and the contents hidden from the children until you are ready to show them. The children will soon get to know that the story basket contains all sorts of exciting toys and visual aids and they will be eager to sit by you, waiting for you to say, 'I wonder what's in the story basket today!' Intrigue them; keep them guessing! Open the lid a fraction and peep in yourself. 'Oh, I can see something very pretty fluttering about... with a tiny body... and two colourful wings... Would you like to see? Yes, it's a bright, beautiful *(bringing out the toy)* BUTTERFLY!'

The 'Story basket' story has been especially written to prepare the children for hearing the Bible story. If you have very young children in the group, however, you may choose to use just this simple story. If so, the words in bold at the end of the section will help you to make the story complete in itself.

Suggested songs

Try to encourage any adults present to join in with the suggested songs. It is quite acceptable to sing nursery rhymes and general songs familiar to everyone, especially when they provide a neat link with your theme. For example, 'The sun has got his hat on' is not a specifically Christian song, but the sun is part of God's creation and could link in with a harvest theme.

The songbooks suggested here are *Okki-tokki-unga*, *Apusskidu* and *Carol, gaily carol* (all published by A&C Black), *Feeling Good!* (published by the National Society/Church House Publishing) and *Junior Praise Combined Edition* (published by Marshall

Pickering). Suggested songs other than in these books are well known and should be easy to locate in compilation songbooks with simple piano accompaniments for very young children. You might also wish to have a selection of tapes of Christian songs, such as *Spring Harvest Kids' Praise 2000*, which are available from your local Christian bookshop. Don't be afraid to play the children short excerpts from classical music. They might skip or sway to rhythmic music, mime conducting or playing a musical instrument, or simply listen quietly with their eyes closed.

Feeling Good! National Society/Church House Publishing, ISBN 0 7151 4850 8
Okki-tokki-unga, A&C Black, ISBN 0 7136 4078 2
Apusskidu, A&C Black, ISBN 0 7136 1846 9
Carol, gaily carol, A&C Black, ISBN 0 7136 579 44
Junior Praise Combined Edition, Marshall Pickering, ISBN 0 551 04014 9
Spring Harvest Kids' Praise 2000, Spring Harvest, music ref ICC43910

Play acting

The 'Play acting' section is really aimed at children who are just starting at school rather than toddlers. They will have fun trying out the mimes and this will help them to be thinking along the right lines before you read them the Bible story.

Nature notes

 In the 'Nature notes' section, suggestions are given for natural objects, plants, insects and animals that you might display to help the children to develop a real interest in the natural world and take note of the changing seasons. Keep some good reference books in the classroom so that together you can identify any birds, flowers, trees and insects they have seen. The children are much more likely to remember the name of something they have helped to identify.

Craft

 The craft page can be photocopied and given to the children to colour or decorate. It can be taken home and displayed as a reminder of everything they have learned in the session. Show the children postcards and prints of famous paintings (from art galleries, calendars or greetings cards) that fit in with the different themes. Some suggestions are given.

Prayer

The prayer is short and simple, tying together all the elements of the session and making them relevant to the children. In a church group, ask a different (willing) adult to read it out each time as a way of including them in the session. (You may find new storytellers or committee members!) Explain to the children that prayer is simply talking to God, but try to instil in them a sense of wonder that the one who made our world is listening to us. Encourage them to keep still and quiet, with their eyes shut and their hands together, for this short time. You may like to introduce the prayer with the traditional rhyme:

> *Teddy bear, Teddy bear,*
> *Turn around.*
> *Teddy bear, Teddy bear,*
> *Touch the ground.*
>
> *Teddy bear, Teddy bear,*
> *Climb the stairs.*
> *Teddy bear, Teddy bear,*
> *Say your prayers!*

Bible story

The Bible story has been especially written for you to read aloud to the children. Show them the pictures as you do so. You may photocopy and enlarge the illustrations if you wish to use them as colouring-in sheets. The stories are often interactive, with suggested mimes to help bring them alive. Encourage the children to repeat any words written in bold (usually amusing words or important phrases). The children will participate more on a second reading.

Ready, Steady, Go!

Where do you begin? First of all, look at the Contents page for an appropriate seasonal topic. Then…

Ready!

Pack the story basket with the items suggested. Try to make sure that these are colourful and appealing to young children. (Some of the parents in your group may be able to lend you toys if you have none at home.)

Steady!

Take the time to read the Bible verses on which the material is based. It will help to focus your mind on the points you want to put across. (The Bible story is based on the first Bible reference in the list.)

Go!

You're ready to provide some *Seasonal fun for the very young*!

Don't forget to advertise the dates, times and place of your meetings by photocopying and enlarging the poster on page 4. Put posters in your local shops, the library and the health centre as well as on your church noticeboards. Give one to whoever runs your baptism preparation classes so that they can recommend your group to the families they meet.

Spring

MOTHERING SUNDAY: LET'S GET BUSY!

Introduction

In this session, the children think about the responsibilities involved in looking after something or someone, before they hear the story of Mary and Joseph looking for the boy Jesus and finding him in the temple.

Ready...

Pack the story basket with whatever toy household items you can find, such as a brush, an iron, pots and pans, a washing-up bowl, a vacuum cleaner and so on.

Steady...

Read Luke 2:41–52; Ephesians 6:1–4

Go...

You're ready to help the children to think about all the things their mums (or carers) do for them and to say 'thank you'.

★ ★ ★

Let's begin!

Welcome

Welcome everyone! Especially…

For the adults

Traditionally, Mothering Sunday was the day when Christians visited their mother church (the most important church or cathedral) halfway through Lent. In Victorian times, the whole family went to church and returned to a special meal. Working children were allowed the day off to visit their mothers. They took with them a gift such as flowers, gloves or a simnel cake. American soldiers who came to Britain during the Second World War revived the idea of a special day for mothers. Cards were designed to show how hard mothers worked in the home.

Notices

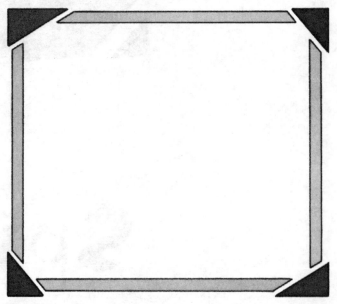

Sing Happy Birthday to...

The story basket

Ask the children whether they ever help with some of the jobs that have to be done at home. Say, 'It's a lot of hard work looking after a family, isn't it? Mrs Bear works very hard looking after Teddy and Little Ted. One day, when the sun is shining brightly, Mrs Bear flings open the windows and sniffs the air. "Mmm, spring is on its way!" she says. "It's time to give the house a spring-clean after the long winter!"'

Teddy asks what spring-cleaning is and, when Mrs Bear explains, he begs her to let him help. Carry on with the story, bringing out the relevant items from the basket for each job that Teddy has to do, and getting the children to mime some of the actions, such as sweeping, stirring a pan, washing and ironing and so on.

Say, 'Teddy is tired at the end of the day and so is Mrs Bear, but she makes Teddy his tea. "Thank you for helping me today," says Mrs Bear. "And thank you for looking after me every day!" says Teddy, running to give his mum a kiss!'

> **And let's say a big thank you to the people who look after us! THANK YOU! God wants us to take special care of our mums (or the people who look after us).**

Suggested songs

Little Bo-peep
Little boy blue
Can you tell me? (*Okki-tokki-unga*)
People we love (*Feeling Good!*)
Thank you for the love (*Junior Praise*)

Listen to 'Spring' from the *Four Seasons* by Vivaldi

Play acting

Provide some dusters and a big rubbish bag and get the children to help you to spring-clean your hall or classroom (or a doll's house) and to tidy the cupboards. You might do this in preparation for asking mums and carers to tea, simnel cake and a 'thank you' song (sung to the tune of 'Daisy, Daisy').

Mummy, Mummy, this is a card / song for you,
Just to thank you for all the things you do.
A mother is very busy,
It makes us feel quite dizzy (roll heads!)
So take a seat, put up your feet,
And we'll bring you a cake / treat or two!

Nature notes

Ask the children to talk about their pets and what they do each day to look after them. Perhaps someone could bring in a hamster to show how the cage should be cleaned.

The birds are busy this month, building their nests. Can the children spot any flying to and fro with bits and bobs in their beaks? Talk about the different places birds choose for their nests (for example, owls in a tree hole, robins in an old kettle or jacket, rooks high up in the trees and so on). Talk about the different materials they use and the shapes of their nests.

Craft

Make Mother's Day cards from the picture on page 15. The children could stick coloured tissue on to the flowers.

Let the children cut out gingerbread ladies from prepared dough and press in currant eyes and buttons. When the biscuits are cooked, add a nose, mouth, dress and apron with white writing-icing.

Prayer

Ask _____ to read today's prayer.

Dear God, thank you for all the people/our mums who love us and look after us. Thank you for loving us too! Amen

Have you seen Jesus?

When Jesus was a baby, his mother Mary was very busy looking after him and taking care of their house. She washed the clothes… and hung them up to dry… *(mime these actions)* She swept the floor… She rocked Jesus to sleep in her arms… and many other things, too!

Mary watched Jesus grow from a baby into a toddler and then a small boy. As each birthday came, Jesus was stronger and taller than the year before. One year, he just fitted under Mary's arm… *(tap under arm)* but when she measured him the following year, he came right up to her shoulder… *(tap shoulder)*

'Why, you will soon be taller than me!' exclaimed Mary, laughing.

But the thing that pleased Mary the most was that Jesus was such a kind and helpful boy.

Sometimes, Jesus seemed just like the other boys in the town. But Mary knew that Jesus was the Son of God. An angel had told her so. And one day, something happened to remind her that Jesus was special.

Every spring, Mary and Joseph packed their bags and took Jesus to visit the temple—the temple was like a big church—in the city of Jerusalem. Lots of other people went too! In the temple, they all said 'thank you' to God for looking after them. Mary told Jesus that the temple was sometimes called God's house.

When Jesus was twelve years old, he went with Mary and Joseph to Jerusalem as usual. On the way there, Jesus met his aunts and uncles, his cousins and his friends all going to Jerusalem too. What fun Jesus had with the other boys, sleeping outside under the stars and playing together.

'Who'll be the first one to see Jerusalem?' shouted one.

'I will!' shouted another. 'But who will be the first one to see the temple?'

When everyone had said 'thank you' to God, it was time to come home again. Mary walked at the front with all the other mothers. Joseph walked at the back with the other fathers and some big boys. At last, Joseph caught up with Mary.

'Where's Jesus?' he asked.

Mary felt her heart sink.

'I thought he was with you!' she cried... *(point to a partner)*

'No!' said Joseph. 'I thought he was with you!' *(point back)*

Mary and Joseph looked for Jesus... *(hand shields eyes)*

They asked the uncles and aunts. 'Have you seen Jesus?'

They asked the cousins. 'Have you seen Jesus?'

They asked all their friends. 'Have you seen Jesus?'

But everyone said, 'No!'

Mary and Joseph were very worried. They didn't know what had happened to Jesus. So they hurried back to Jerusalem to look for him.

They looked for him in the streets...

They looked for him in the market place... and in the house where they had been staying. But they couldn't find him anywhere.

'Where could he be?' said Mary. *(Ask the children to guess.)*

After three whole days of searching, they went into the temple—and *there* was Jesus! He was sitting with all the temple teachers, learning about God.

He listened to the teachers... *(cup ear)*

He talked to the teachers... *(make hands talk)*

And everyone was amazed at the sensible things that he said—for he was only twelve years old.

But Mary couldn't keep quiet any longer.

'Jesus!' she said. 'We didn't know where you were! We've been searching *everywhere* for you!'

'Why didn't you look in the temple first?' asked Jesus. 'I thought you would guess that I was in my Father's house!'

'Come on!' said Joseph kindly. 'It's time to go home!' So Jesus did as he was told and said 'goodbye' to the teachers until the following year. But Mary never forgot the time when they searched everywhere for Jesus and found him in the temple— God's house! Why do you think they found him there?

A card for Mother's Day

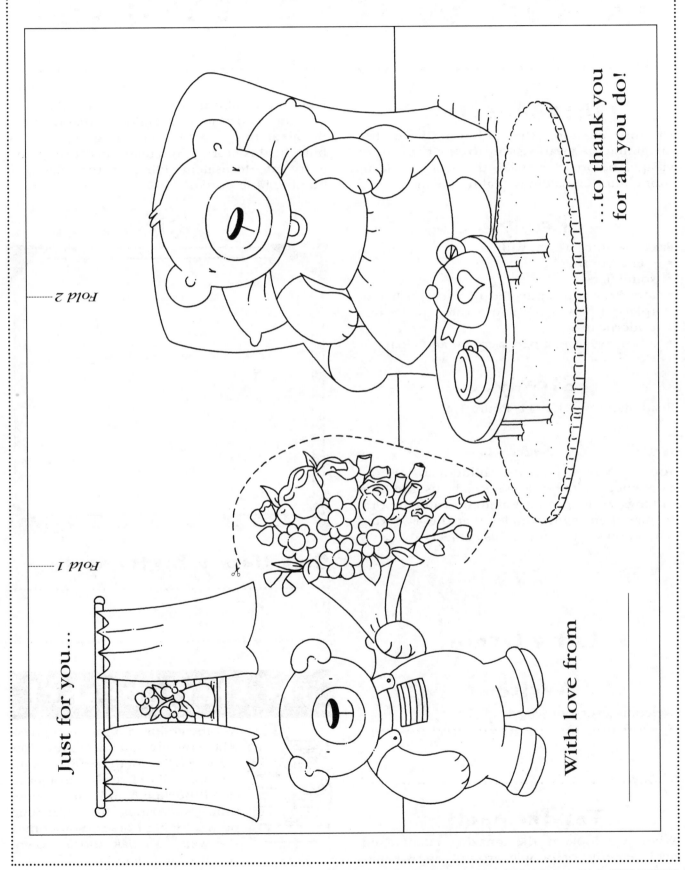

Fold 2

Fold 1

...to thank you
for all you do!

Just for you...

With love from

_____

PALM SUNDAY: LOOK WHO'S COMING!

Introduction

In this session, the children have fun imagining a royal visitor to their town or village, before they hear the story of Jesus riding into Jerusalem on Palm Sunday.

Ready...

Pack the story basket with:

• some bunting
• some flags
• Mrs Bear with Little Ted in a toy pushchair (place a baby's bib and a ruler in the tray underneath)
• a bear wearing a paper crown and cloak

Steady...

Read Matthew 21:1–11; Psalm 139

Go...

You're ready to help the children to feel the excitement of the onlookers as Jesus, the King of kings, rode into Jerusalem on Palm Sunday. Inspire them with wonder that this is a king who knows every one of his subjects.

★ ★ ★

Let's begin!

Welcome

Welcome everyone! Especially…

For the adults

When we look at the amazing talents and achievements of people around us, we may feel humble about our own. Perhaps the story of Palm Sunday should remind us that God can do great things with whatever gifts we offer him. In this story, Jesus made his triumphant entry into Jerusalem riding on the back of a humble little donkey.

Notices

Sing Happy Birthday to...

The story basket

Ask the children if they can guess who you are talking about. Her name is Elizabeth. She lives in London. She lives in a palace called Buckingham Palace. Sometimes she rides in a carriage pulled by big horses. Sometimes she wears a cloak and a crown. Yes, it's the Queen!

Make up a story about Teddy seeing the Queen Bear drive through his town or village. Build up the anticipation and excitement! One day, Teddy is out shopping with Mrs Bear and Little Ted. Mrs Bear is having trouble with the pushchair because there are so many people standing on the pavement. They all seem to be waiting for someone. Teddy sees that the shops have decorations all along the fronts *(hang up the bunting)*. Whoever is coming must be very important!

He looks up the road and sees some motorcycles and a big black car coming along very slowly. Could it be? Yes! It's the Queen Bear driving into Teddy's town. Get everyone to shout, 'Hooray! Here comes the Queen! Three cheers for the Queen!' Teddy sees that lots of people are waving flags *(give some to the children to wave)*. Now he wants something to wave at the Queen. Mrs Bear looks in the bottom of the pushchair and finds one of Little Ted's spare bibs and a ruler. She ties the bib to the ruler. When the Queen goes by, she smiles at Teddy's special flag and gives a royal wave *(ask everyone to give a royal wave!)*. Teddy is very pleased.

When they get home, Teddy asks Mrs Bear if the Queen knows him. Mrs Bear shakes her head.

> **The Queen doesn't know all the people who live in her country, but Jesus, the King of kings, knows each one of us!**

Suggested songs

Pussy cat, pussy cat, where have you been?
This is the way the ladies ride (see 'Play acting' below)
Ferdinando, the donkey (*Apusskidu*)
We have a king who rides a donkey (*Junior Praise*)
National anthems

Play the Hallelujah Chorus from Handel's *Messiah*

Play acting

Small children love bouncing on their parents' knees for:

This is the way the ladies ride,
trit trot, trit trot, trit trot! (bounce gently)
This is the way the gentlemen ride, gallop,
gallop, gallop! (bounce slightly higher)
This is the way the farmers ride, hobblety-
hoy, hobblety-hoy! (bounce higher still)

Over the gate (raise child up)
And down into a ditch! (allow child to fall gently between your open knees, before bringing him or her back into your arms)

Practise walking, trotting and galloping around the room to suitable music.

The children line up facing one another as a boy and a girl walk down the middle, pretending to be a king and queen. The children bow or curtsey as they pass.

Nature notes

Make a right royal display of golden flowers such as daffodils, primroses, polyanthuses and kingcups.

Cut some stems of pussy willow—the grey fur on the male buds is now producing bright yellow heads of fluffy 'palm'.

Look who's coming in the way of birds arriving for the summer (house martins, swifts, cuckoos and so on) and look what's coming on the fruit trees—blossom that will turn into summer fruit.

You may like to consider adopting a donkey from a donkey sanctuary as a class project.

Craft

Cut out the donkey on page 21. Let the children stick the ears on the donkey and add wool of different lengths for the mane. With older children, attach the ears with split pins and ask them to move the ears backwards and forwards as you read the story on page 18.

Alternatively, make flags by decorating rectangles of paper and gluing one end to a dowel rod. Wave them in a set pattern to a song such as 'Joy is the flag' (*Junior Praise*).

Prayer

Ask _____ to read today's prayer.

Thank you, King Jesus, that you know us and we can get to know you.

Thank you that we can learn all about you in Bible stories and talk to you when we pray. Please help us to know you better every day. Amen

Look who's coming!

There was once a little donkey who lived with his mother in a village not far from Jerusalem. The little donkey was beautiful. He had big brown eyes and long, pointed ears that he could move backwards and forwards…

When he was feeling happy or interested, he put his ears right forward…

But when he was frightened or cross, he put his ears right back… until they lay almost flat along his fluffy mane.

The little donkey was so young that no one had ridden on his back yet. But he didn't mind. He was very happy to wander under the olive trees or gallop over the hillside and look across at the shining rooftops of Jerusalem on the hill opposite. Sometimes, the man who owned him was worried that he would get lost and so he used to tie the little donkey to a tree with an old piece of rope.

One day, as the two donkeys stood side by side, they heard voices. The little donkey put his ears right forward…

'Look who's coming!' he said to his mother.

Two men looked over the gate. They had smiling faces and stripy cloaks.

'There's the little donkey Jesus was telling us about!' they said, jumping over the gate.

'What a lovely little fellow you are!'

The men untied the rope and opened the gate. The little donkey put his ears back…

'What's happening?' he asked his mother. 'I don't belong to these men.' Then he lifted his head, opened his mouth and brayed so loudly that he could be heard all around the village. EE-AW! EE-AW!

At this, the owner looked out of his window.

'Hey, what are you doing with my little donkey?' he called.

The two men spoke up politely.

'Jesus, our Master, needs him!' said one of the men.

'But he'll send him back again soon!' explained the other.

'Did you say Jesus?' asked the owner. 'Then you may carry on. Trot on, little donkey! You'll be quite safe with Jesus!'

The little donkey trotted along the road beside the men with the stripy cloaks. It was quite an adventure and he put his ears right forward again…

'Who is Jesus?' he asked some noisy sparrows in a tree.

'Why, Jesus is the Son of God!' they chirped. 'He takes good care of all God's creatures, even small birds like us!'

'I wonder what he wants with me,' thought the little donkey.

When they had left the village behind, the little donkey was surprised to see lots of people standing all along the road. He wasn't used to being in a crowd and he felt frightened by all the noise and excitement. Back went his ears… until they lay almost flat along his mane. But a man with kind eyes stepped out of the crowd and came towards him.

'Don't be frightened!' he whispered in the little donkey's ears. 'I asked my friends to bring you to me. Will you carry me on your back all along the road and into Jerusalem?'

At once, the little donkey felt happy and peaceful. He stood quite still to let the men put their stripy cloaks over him and to let Jesus climb on to his back. Then, with his ears right forward… he set off along the road that led to Jerusalem.

'Look who's coming!' shouted the people. 'It's Jesus, our gentle king, riding on a donkey!'

As they walked through the crowd, the little donkey heard everything the people were saying.

'Jesus made my sister better!' shouted a boy.

'He told us a lovely story!' called some children.

And the more he heard, the more the little donkey felt proud to be carrying Jesus on his back.

'Hosanna!' shouted the people on either side of him. They waved branches of palm trees and laid their cloaks upon the ground for the little donkey to walk over. But now he wasn't worried by all the noise and excitement. His ears stayed pointing forward… and he just kept walking up the road and through the gates into the city of Jerusalem.

We have a King who rides a donKey!

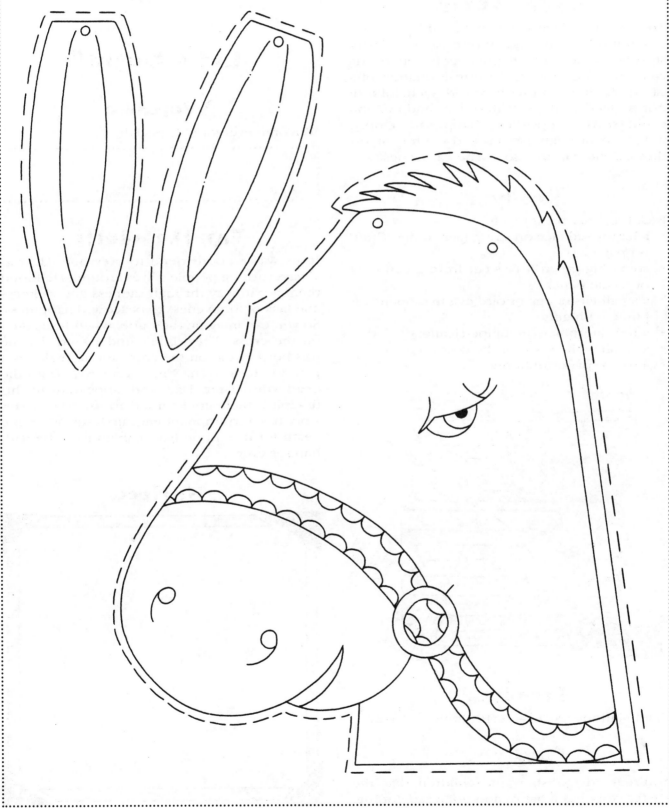

EASTER: CHEER UP!

Introduction

This session forms the basis of an Easter celebration for your group or class. The Easter story is a difficult one to put over to very young children. The story of the transformation of a caterpillar into a butterfly provides a helpful (if not perfect) analogy. With older children, you could revise 'opposites' (happy/sad, empty/full, dead/alive, and so on) and see how many they can hear in the story 'The Easter nest'.

Ready...

Pack the story basket with:

- a happy/sad face on string (see under 'Craft' on page 24)
- some big green leaves cut from green card or tissue paper
- a small Easter egg or card egg that opens for filling with gifts
- a toy caterpillar (or a pipe-cleaner)
- a small white sock for the cocoon
- a toy or paper butterfly

Steady...

Read Matthew 26:14—28:10; John 16:16–22

Go...

You're ready to show the children that the Easter story has a happy and not a sad ending.

★ ★ ★

Let's begin!

Welcome

Welcome everyone! Especially…

For the adults

Jesus was a good friend to everyone. He was always turning people's lives around. He found them a pathway through sadness and sickness and lack of forgiveness to peace and happiness. So you can imagine their grief when Jesus died on the cross. They didn't understand that he was born to die on the cross and to make us a pathway to heaven. When Jesus rose from the dead on Easter Day and appeared to his disciples, their grief turned to joy. The Easter story has a triumphant ending. Jesus overcame death for us and he has enabled us to be with him for ever.

Notices

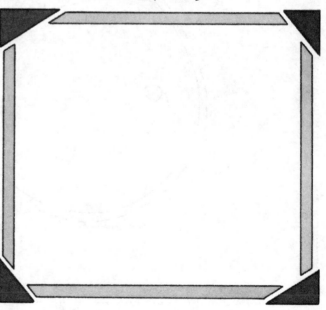

....

....

The story basket

Read to the children as follows.

Welcome to our Easter celebration, everyone! *(Bring out the sad/happy face.)* Here's a sad face... and a happy face. A sad face... and a happy face. Can you look sad? Now slowly turn your faces into happy faces. Make your smiles bigger and bigger until they stretch from one ear to the other! That's good! There's a lot to be happy about at this time of year. Have you seen... *(mention spring flowers, blossom, lambs, as appropriate)*? So let's sing a song about being happy/springtime. *(See page 24 for suggested songs.)*

Teddy wants me to tell you a story with a happy ending. So come and sit by the story basket and I'll tell you the story of the beautiful butterfly.

One day, a beautiful butterfly came floating down into a garden... *(link thumbs and flutter fingers)*. It landed on the big green leaf of a stinging nettle, and there it laid an egg... *(bring out the Easter egg)*. Inside the egg, something was growing. I wonder what that was! A tiny creature that grew bigger and bigger until the eggshell cracked and out popped a hairy, stripy caterpillar! Can you make one finger wiggle like a caterpillar?

'I feel hungry!' said the caterpillar, and he began to munch the nettle leaf, munch, munch, until there was nothing left of it at all.

'I'm *still* hungry,' said the caterpillar, and he wriggled his way on to another juicy leaf and began to munch again. How did he eat? *Munch, munch, munch!*

Very soon, the little caterpillar grew into a great big caterpillar. He was a very good friend to all the other caterpillars in the garden. He showed them where to find the biggest, juiciest leaves, and he told them how to wave their tails in the air to frighten away the hungry birds, swish, swish! No wonder all the caterpillars in the nettle patch loved him so much!

But one sad day, the caterpillar told his friends, 'I'm sorry, but I must go away now to do something very special.'

'Oh, don't go away and leave us!' cried the other caterpillars. 'Who will show us where to find the biggest, juiciest leaves, and who will help us to scare the birds away? And anyway, we love you and we don't want to be without you—not now, not ever!'

'I really must go!' said the caterpillar. 'But don't be sad! I promise you'll see me again and then you'll be very glad!'

The caterpillar wriggled his way up a bumpy tree trunk. Then he began to make himself a silky sleeping bag called a cocoon... *(bring out the sock)*. He snuggled down inside the cocoon, pulled it over his head and disappeared from sight... *(put the caterpillar inside the sock)*. When the other caterpillars saw that their friend had gone, they went away sadly.

Inside the cocoon, the caterpillar began to change. He wriggled out of his stripy, hairy body... *(all wriggle)* and then he grew long legs and silky wings... *(all flap arms)* and he burst out of the cocoon as a beautiful, colourful butterfly... *(show butterfly)*.

As he was drying his wings in the sun, his caterpillar friends found the empty cocoon and started to cry.

'Oh dear, where has our special friend gone?' they cried. 'The hungry birds must have eaten him. Now we'll never see him again.'

'Why are you crying?' asked the new butterfly. 'Are you looking for me?'

The caterpillars looked round.

'It's you!' they cried. 'You've come back! But look at you! Now you're a beautiful, colourful butterfly!'

'A good friend always keeps his promise!' laughed the butterfly. 'Don't forget, I'll always be your friend. One day, you'll be butterflies too and then we'll float above the nettle patch—together for ever!' *(all make hands into butterflies again)*.

Suggested songs

If you're happy and you know it (*Apusskidu*)

A happy time of year (*Feeling Good!*)

Thank you, Lord, for this fine day (*Junior Praise*)

Morning has broken (*Junior Praise*)

Creepy, crawly caterpillar (*Feeling Good!*)

If I were a butterfly (*Junior Praise*)

All things bright and beautiful (*Junior Praise*)

Jesus lives again (*Feeling Good!*)

One, two, three, Jesus loves me (*Junior Praise*)

Roll the stone (*Junior Praise*)

Jesus' love is very wonderful (*Junior Praise*)

Play acting

Carry on the theme of 'opposites' by inviting the children to perform opposites with their bodies, such as curling up into a ball and then stretching high into the air, sitting very still and then jumping up and down, and practising their happy and sad faces.

Nature notes

Carry on the theme of 'opposites' by charting the changeable spring weather—one minute warm and sunny and the next cold with an April shower. Who can spot a rainbow? Cloud formations are dramatic this month. Now it gets light early and dark late.

Open up a book showing the life cycle of a butterfly. If you bring any caterpillars indoors, make sure that they come with some of the leaves of the plant on which you found them.

Craft

Pencil in a sad and a happy face on either side of a small circle of card for the children to draw over. Punch holes on both sides of the card, as shown, and tie a short length of string to each.

Make the face turn from sad to happy by twisting the string. (You will need to draw one face the opposite way up to the other.)

Prayer

Ask _____ to read today's prayer.

Dear God, Easter is such a happy time of year! Everywhere we can see winter turning into spring. We thank you for blossom on the trees, for nests full of eggs, for the bright colours of spring flowers and butterflies' wings. Thank you for our friends, who help us to enjoy your beautiful world. But most of all, thank you for Jesus, who has promised to be our friend for ever. Amen

The Easter nest

Two swallows were chattering in a quiet garden.

'It's springtime!' sang Long-tail to his wife. 'Shall we build a nest in the tree beside this empty cave?'

'Oh, yes!' said Short-tail. 'Wouldn't it be fun to have a nest full of baby swallows?'

The two swallows flew backwards and forwards, bringing mud to build their nest. As they worked, the nest grew bigger and bigger until it was the size of a cup balanced between the branches.

'I'm very hungry,' said Short-tail when the nest was finished at last. 'Let's fly over the city walls into Jerusalem to find some food.'

The birds soon spotted some breadcrumbs on a window sill.

'Eat up, my dear!' said Long-tail.

But Short-tail was looking through the window into an upstairs room.

'Look! It's our friend Jesus!' she cried happily. 'The person who looks after small birds like us. He's having some supper with his friends.'

Suddenly, one of the men with Jesus left the room.

'That's Judas,' said Long-tail. 'He has an angry look on his face. I wonder what he's going to do?'

It was getting late now, but the two swallows were worried about their friend Jesus. So they followed him into a garden called the garden of Gethsemane.

'Please stay awake while I pray,' Jesus begged his friends.

But they were much too sleepy and they soon fell asleep. Then Judas brought some Roman soldiers into the garden. They took hold of Jesus and marched him away.

Long-tail was angry.

'So that's what Judas was up to!' he said. 'I thought he was supposed to be Jesus' friend.'

Early the next morning, the swallows found Jesus at the palace. A crowd of angry people were shouting, 'Kill him! Take him away and kill him!'

'Why do they want to kill Jesus?' asked Short-tail. 'He is so gentle and kind.'

'They don't believe he is the Son of God,' explained Long-tail.

'But he *is* the Son of God!' exclaimed Short-tail. 'He is the King of kings.'

The swallows flew down to try to help Jesus, but a soldier waved his sword at them and frightened them away.

Long-tail took Short-tail back to the quiet garden.

'You were very brave!' he said proudly. 'But now you must be braver still.'

Short-tail looked down the path. She saw that the soldiers were making Jesus carry a heavy cross up the hill. He often slipped and fell.

'What are they going to do to him?' she whispered.

'I'm afraid they are going to kill Jesus,' said Long-tail.

The soldiers put Jesus on the cross in between two other crosses. They left him there to die. Then the sky turned black and the ground shook. The two swallows hid their heads under their wings.

In the evening, a kind man called Joseph came to put Jesus' body in the cave. Then he rolled a big stone in front of the cave to close it tight. And for a long time, the swallows heard a lady called Mary crying in the garden.

The next day, nobody came to the garden. The swallows sat beside the big stone, feeling very gloomy.

'Cheer up!' said Long-tail.

'I can't,' said Short-tail. 'Jesus is dead! Who will look after the birds now?'

As soon as the first sunbeams danced into the garden on Sunday morning, the swallows woke up and saw that the cave was open. The stone was rolled to one side. They fluttered inside the cave, but they were surprised to see that it was empty.

'Don't worry!' said an angel with white feathery wings. 'Jesus has come back to life. He is alive!'

The swallows flew back into the sunshine. Mary was looking into the empty cave and she was crying again.

'Are you looking for me, Mary?' asked a man who was standing behind her. Mary looked round. Then she stopped crying and began to smile. It was Jesus!

'Jesus is alive! He's alive!' sang the two swallows, full of joy.

And very soon, Long-tail and Short-tail were the proud parents of four baby swallows, all opening their beaks for more food in their beautiful Easter nest.

Decorated eggs

Use yellow ribbon to hang the decorated egg shapes on a bunch of twigs.

Summer

PENTECOST: WHERE'S MY BLANKET?

●●

Introduction

Ask the children to bring in any objects that comfort them, such as an old blanket or a favourite soft toy. This is a good 'way in' to the story of Pentecost, when the disciples received the promised Holy Spirit to comfort and inspire them.

Ready...

Pack the story basket with:

- a cot quilt or blanket
- Teddy's overnight bag
- Teddy's pyjamas
- Teddy's sponge bag, flannel and toothbrush

Steady...

Read Luke 24:36–53; Acts 2; John 14:15–31; Matthew 28:16–20

Go...

You're ready to explain that Jesus is with us always (through his Holy Spirit).

★ ★ ★

Let's begin!

Welcome

Welcome everyone! Especially…

For the adults

Explain that the disciples received the Holy Spirit on the day of Pentecost—a day seven weeks after the Passover festival, when the Jews gave thanks for the first ripe crops. God wants our lives to 'bear fruit'. Let us be set alight with enthusiasm for new projects that will help others in our communities.

Notices

Sing Happy Birthday to...

The story basket

Ask the children to show the special blanket or toy they have brought in and to tell everyone about it. Does it have a name? Explain that Teddy has a special blanket called 'Patch' *(bring it out)* that he always holds on to when he goes to sleep at night. He had it on his cot when he was a baby and although it is getting very old and untidy, Teddy still loves it.

Make up a story about Teddy going to stay the night with a friend for the first time. Teddy is very excited about staying the night at his friend's house. He packs the things he will need to take with him into his bag. Can you help him? *(Bring out the items one by one and ask different children to pack them in the bag.)* Teddy has a lovely time playing with his friend and having tea. At bedtime, he puts on

his pyjamas, brushes his teeth, washes his face and climbs into bed. But Teddy can't get to sleep. He turns this way and that way. No! Something is wrong! Can you guess what it is? Yes, Teddy has forgotten to bring 'Patch', his favourite blanket, with him.

Finish the story by saying that Teddy is very sensible because he tells his friend's mummy and she telephones Mrs Bear, who brings the blanket. Teddy is very pleased to see it and is soon fast asleep.

> **Although we can't see him, Jesus is always with us, helping us to feel safe and to be brave and sensible.**

Suggested songs

I whistle a happy tune (*Apusskidu*)
A windmill in old Amsterdam (*Apusskidu*)
Candle time (*Feeling Good!*)
Away in a manger (last verse only) (*Junior Praise*)
I'm very glad of God (*Junior Praise*)

Sing a simple song in another language, such as *Frère Jacques* or *Kum-Ba-Ya*. Think about wind instruments and listen to a trumpet voluntary.

Play acting

Luke 24:36–49 is full of different emotions experienced by the disciples when Jesus appears to them. Talk about the meaning of *startled*, *frightened*, *amazed* and *joyful*. Mime a simple story about taking a favourite toy to the park to play, walking home and being *startled* to discover that the toy has gone missing, going back to look for it and being *amazed* to find it before *joyfully* taking it home.

Nature notes

May is a wonderful month for flowers. If possible, take the children for a walk to see blankets of bluebells, buttercups or daisies in woods, fields or parks. Two flowers to identify that would fit in well with the theme are the forget-me-not and the speedwell. The latter grows alongside fields and roads as if to speed you well on your journey! Inspire the children with a love of flowers by allowing them to arrange what they have found in jam jars.

Make a 'comfort bag' for the birds by stuffing an old net bag with bits of wool, fluff, dead leaves, dried moss, feathers, string, hair and straw. Hang it on a tree and watch the birds come to peck out bits and pieces to make and line their nests.

Craft

Look at Impressionist paintings of summer and flowers such as *The Poppy Field* by Claude Monet or *A Girl with a Watering Can* by Auguste Renoir.

Make a paper patchwork quilt by giving everyone a hexagonal shape and asking them to draw or glue on it a picture of people or objects that help them, keep them safe or inspire them. Put the shapes together and make 'stitches' with a felt-tip pen.

Cut out two strips of thin card for the windmill on the craft sheet (on page 35) and secure them in place with a split pin.

Prayer

Ask _____ to read today's prayer.

Thank you, Jesus, that you never forget us. You are always with us, helping us to feel safe and making us feel brave. Please help us to do things that make you happy and proud. Amen

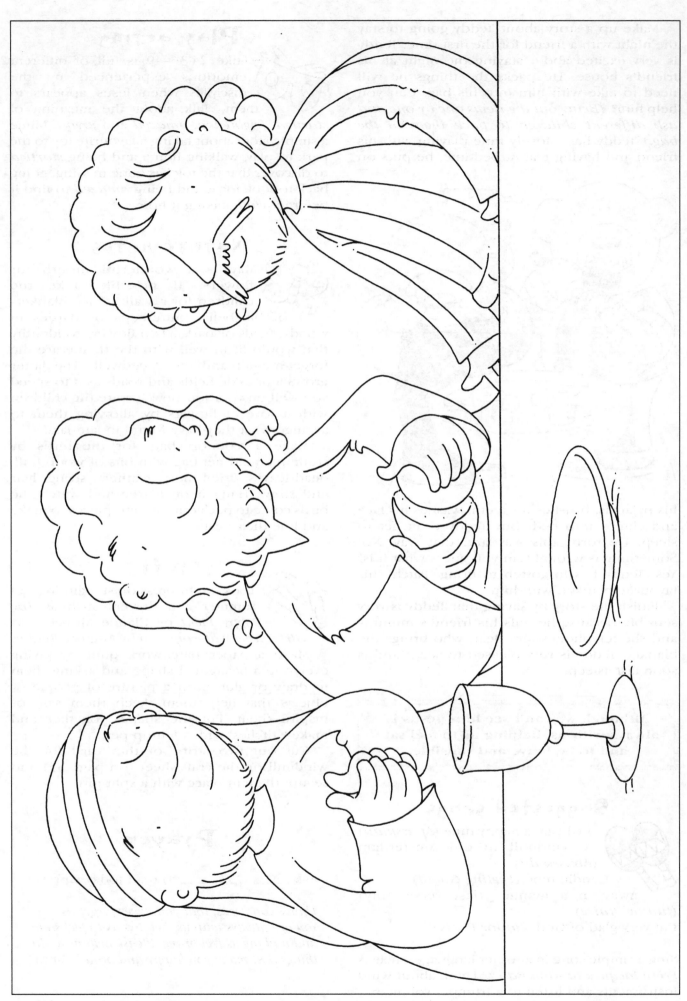

The special helper

Do you remember the story of Easter? Jesus died on the cross and all his friends were very sad. They laid his body in a cave in a beautiful garden. Then they closed the cave with a big stone. But on Easter Sunday, Mary went walking in the garden and she saw that the cave was open. Somebody called her name. She looked round and saw Jesus standing in the garden.

'Mary!' he said. 'Go and tell my friends that I am alive!'

How happy Mary must have felt. She couldn't wait to run all the way back down the path into Jerusalem to tell her friends the wonderful news.

But no one believed Mary!

'I can't believe Jesus is alive,' said one. 'Mary must be making a mistake.'

'Jesus died,' said another. 'He *can't* be alive!'

All of a sudden, they looked up and saw that Jesus was standing right there in the room with them. They felt very frightened because they didn't expect to see him.

'Don't be afraid!' said Jesus.

'Look! It's me!'

'Jesus, it really is you!' they cried joyfully. 'Mary was right! You *are* alive!'

Jesus sat down to have supper with his friends. He told them that soon he would be going home to heaven to be with God.

'When I have gone, I want you to take good care of one another,' he said. 'And I want you to tell everyone all about me.'

'But what shall we say?' asked his friends. 'We're not very good at speaking up.'

'Don't worry!' said Jesus. 'I'm going to send you a special helper, called the Holy Spirit, who will tell you what to say and help you to speak up bravely.'

Just before he went back to heaven, Jesus went for a walk with his friends up a steep hill.

'Thank you for being such good friends to me,' said Jesus. 'And don't forget, I'll always be with you, even though you can't see me.'

Then he went up into the sky. His friends watched until a

blanket of cloud hid him from their eyes.

Jesus' friends went back to Jerusalem to wait for the special helper, the Holy Spirit, to come. They wondered what he would be like. Would the Holy Spirit really make them feel brave enough to stand up in front of a crowd of people and tell them all about Jesus?

One Sunday, the friends found out. It happened on a day called the day of Pentecost, when Jerusalem was full of people from all over the world. They had come to say 'thank you' to God for the harvest fruit and vegetables. As the friends were singing songs and praying together in a house, they heard a noise from the sky that sounded like a strong wind blowing. But the sound wasn't *outside*; it was *inside*, and it seemed to fill the whole house. Then they saw what looked like flickering flames—like bright red butterflies dancing in the air. Each flame came down and rested gently for a moment on each one of the friends.

At once, the friends felt brave and full of joy. They could feel that Jesus was with them, even though they couldn't see him.

'Oh, thank you for sending us the Holy Spirit!' they cried. 'Now we can do anything that God wants us to do.'

And they did! The Holy Spirit helped Jesus' friends to tell people everywhere that God loves us and that Jesus is our friend. They started by telling all the people who were visiting Jerusalem. And do you know, they found that they could talk in many different languages. Everyone could understand what they were saying. Wasn't that amazing?

Welcome to our windmill!

The Spirit is like the wind that blows wherever it wants to. You can hear the wind, but you don't know where it comes from or where it is going (John 3:8).

Reproduced with permission from *Easy Ways to Seasonal Fun for the Very Young* published by BRF 2004 (1 84101 342 0)

PICNIC TIME!

•••

Introduction

This session contains ideas for a friendly summer picnic with your group or class in the park, recreation ground or vicarage garden. Use the invitation on page 48 to invite everybody (including potential new members for the following September) and to find out how many people will be attending. The activities encourage the children to think about being a good friend and lead into the story of Jesus befriending Zacchaeus.

Ready...

If the group are going to bring their own sandwiches and drinks, decide what extra items you might provide—for example, cherry tomatoes, crisps, cocktail sausages, diced cheese, raisins, tray bakes and biscuits. Ice some fairy cakes and decorate them with smiling faces, using small sweets and writing-icing. Provide muffins cut in half and let the children make their own friendly faces, using diced vegetables and raisins.

You may wish to borrow some ride-on toys from a local playgroup and put up an awning if it is going to be very sunny.

If you want an 'ice-breaker' for the adults, ask them all for a small piece of information about themselves in advance. Write out a quiz based on these snippets—for example:

- Who plays the trumpet?
- Which two mothers have twin sisters?
- Who helps with the Rainbows/Beavers?

Pack the story basket with these picnic items for Teddy and his friends.
- a rug
- a doll's hamper or lunch box containing:
  - a drink
  - a sandwich
  - a cake
  - a piece of fruit

Steady...

Read Luke 19:1–10

Go...

You're ready to help the children understand that people can change for the better when we are kind to them.

Let's begin!

Before everyone arrives, set up a teddy bears' picnic with the items from your story basket for the children to see. Ask them to put out their own picnics on rugs and make sure that no one is sitting alone. Before you start eating, ask everyone to gather round Teddy.

Welcome

Welcome everyone, especially those who have come along for the first time today. Tell them all about your group.

For the adults

Give out the quiz and explain that you will be giving out the answers at the end of the picnic. People may be surprised at the things they didn't know about one another. There is always more to learn about God. But, like Zacchaeus, we need to put ourselves in a position where he can speak to us.

Notices

Remind everyone about the summer pram service *(see next session)*.

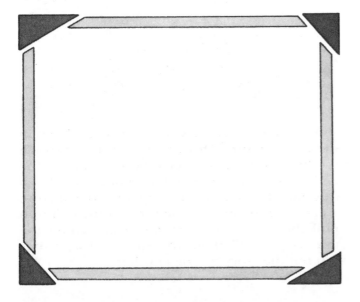

Sing Happy Birthday to...

The story basket

Ask the children if they are looking forward to their picnic. Tell them that Teddy is very excited about eating his lunch outside with his friends. He can't wait to see what is in his picnic basket. Shall we open it and find out? *(Take out the items one by one, drawing attention to the friendly face on a cake, or making Teddy design his own on a muffin.)* A picnic wouldn't be any fun without our friends, would it? Encourage the children to be good friends to one another today by sharing, playing together and saying 'hello' to anyone new. Sing a song or say grace before you eat.

Suggested songs

Picnic time! (sung to the tune of 'Hot cross buns')

Picnic time! Picnic time!
Thank you, God, for food and friends
at picnic time.
Try to be a good friend, smile at someone new.
There'll be fun for everyone at picnic time!

The teddy bears' picnic
Polly put the kettle on
You are welcome (*Feeling Good!*)
Zacchaeus (*Feeling Good!*)
Zacchaeus was a very little man (*Junior Praise*)
The finger-rhyme 'Two fat gentlemen met in a lane' as follows:

Two fat gentlemen met in a lane,
Bowed most politely, bowed once again.
How do you do? How do you do?
How do you do again?

Two thin ladies met in a lane...

Two tall policemen met in a lane...

Two little schoolboys met in a lane...

Two little babies met in a lane...

The 'fat gentlemen' are the thumbs, the 'thin ladies' are the index fingers and so on. Hold up both fists with the thumbs raised and the other fingers closed. Then bend the thumbs slowly forwards as if bowing to one another. Repeat with the other fingers (this is very difficult with the ring finger!).

Play acting

Have fun miming the different ways that people greet one another around the world (shaking hands, bowing, rubbing noses, kissing both

cheeks). Can the children think up any funny, new ideas? Think of all the words we use to greet others (hello, hi, good morning) and learn some in other languages.

Play games that everyone can join in, such as 'The Hokey Cokey'.

Ask two children to hold hands and skip about while everyone sings 'Lou, lou, skip to me, lou' or another lively verse. When you call 'Make friends!' the two children split up and each find a new partner to skip with them. Continue until everyone is skipping.

Nature notes

Go for a nature walk to collect leaves, twigs and pine cones. Remind the children how bare the trees were in the winter and point out how leafy they are now. Notice the different temperatures in the sun and in the shade of the trees. Collect and identify as many different leaves as you can. Point out the veins and the different colours on the top and underside. Are they hairy? Talk about the parts of a tree—the roots, the trunk, the branches and twigs. Look for any insects, animals or plants (such as ivy) climbing the trees.

Craft

Show famous paintings with beautiful trees in them, such as Constable's *Flatford Mill on the River Stour*.

Do bark rubbings with white paper and wax crayons. Preserve the leaves you collected by brushing them with PVC glue and save them for the next session, together with the twigs and pine cones.

Photocopy the craft sheet on page 42, and cut out the rectangle at the top, with Zacchaeus inside it. Make three holes where

shown, one above Zacchaeus' head and two in the tree picture. Thread some string through the hole above Zacchaeus' head and knot the end to secure. Thread the other end down through the bottom hole in the tree picture and out of the hole at the top. Let the children pull the string to make Zacchaeus climb the tree as you tell them the story. Perhaps they can tell the story to one another.

Prayer

Ask _____ to read today's prayer.

Dear God, thank you for the joys of a summer picnic! It's such fun to eat food outside with our friends. Please help us to be good friends to everyone, just like Jesus. Help us to let other people join in with our games and conversations. Amen

A friend for Zacchaeus

There was once a man called Zacchaeus. He lived in a beautiful city called Jericho that was full of trees. There were fruit trees and trees that smelled like perfume and trees with spiky leaves that waved about in the breeze… *(wave arms above heads)*.

Now Zacchaeus had a very good job in Jericho. He had to collect money from all the people who lived in the city and give it to the Roman rulers. As well as a good job, he had a big house and lots of money. He was rich! The only thing that Zacchaeus *didn't* have was a lot of friends. In fact, he didn't have any friends at all. No one liked Zacchaeus very much because sometimes he put the money that he collected into his *own* pockets. That wasn't very honest, was it?

At first, Zacchaeus enjoyed sitting at his table, counting all the coins that he had stolen: '… a hundred and thirty-one, a hundred and thirty-two…'.

But after a while, he began to feel rather lonely. He could hear children playing in the trees outside his window and that made him feel lonelier still.

'This money isn't much good!' he said. 'It doesn't talk to me or ask me how I am feeling today. Something's wrong here. I must make a change! But who will help me? I don't have a friend in the whole wide world.'

As Zacchaeus sat all alone in his house, he heard the children talking excitedly.

'Jesus is coming here today!' said one.

'I know,' said the other. 'I can't wait to see him! My mum says that he is everybody's friend.'

When Zacchaeus heard this, he sat up in his chair. What did the children say? A man called Jesus! A friend to everyone! Coming here today! This was too good to miss. He would go and see what Jesus was like.

Outside, everyone was waiting for Jesus.

'Look! Here he comes!' shouted a boy. 'Hello, Jesus!'

Zacchaeus tried to see over the heads of the people in front, but he was too short. He couldn't

see a thing. He tried to push his way to the front, but no one would let him through. Oh dear, he wouldn't see Jesus at all.

Zacchaeus looked along the road. If only he was as tall as those trees… and that's when he had an idea. Can you guess what it was? Yes! Zacchaeus ran ahead until he found a fig tree. It had a grey trunk and leaves shaped like hands. Quickly, he pulled himself up on to a strong branch. Ah, that was much better. Now he could see Jesus walking towards him.

Zacchaeus gazed at Jesus. He was smiling and talking to everyone. How lovely to have a friend like that! But that was impossible. No one wanted to be *his* friend. Jesus was getting closer. At any moment, he would walk right underneath the fig tree. Zacchaeus peered down through the leaves… and gasped. Jesus was smiling right up at him.

'Zacchaeus, come on down!' he said. 'I'm coming to your house today.'

Zacchaeus slid down the trunk and landed with a bump in front of Jesus. Leafy twigs stuck out of his hair.

'My house is this way,' he said, smiling shyly.

The people in the crowd began to grumble.

'Jesus shouldn't go to *his* house,' they muttered. 'Zacchaeus is a bad man.'

But people can change if someone is kind to them. And that's exactly what Zacchaeus did when Jesus made friends with him that day.

'I'm sorry I've been so selfish,' said Zacchaeus. 'From now on, I'm going to share, and I'm going to give back all the money that I stole from the people of Jericho.'

Jesus was very pleased. And Zacchaeus was pleased, too. He was quite happy to say 'goodbye' to all that money. Why? Because he knew that he would soon be saying 'hello' to lots of new friends. And that was worth more than the tallest pile of coins in the world.

Make Zacchaeus climb the tree!

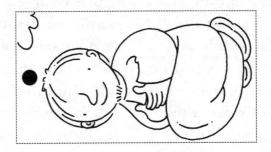

TODDLER PRAISE: TIME FOR A STORY!

Introduction

This session forms the basis of a toddler praise or summer pram service and is a good way to introduce the children to a church service. Keep it short and use a 'small is beautiful' theme to link in with the story of Jesus blessing the little children.

Ready...

Check that the service is in the church diary. Invite the minister to take some part in the service, perhaps welcoming everyone to the church and giving the blessing.

(Give the group's name)

TODDLER PRAISE!

(Give date)

Welcome and introduction

Hymn or song

Reading: Mark 10:13–16

Hymn or song

Story: Jesus welcomes the little children
Hymn or song

(You could explain the meaning of the Bible passage here, before the children come forward to place their photographs around the picture of Jesus)

Hymn or song

Prayer

Blessing

HAPPY SUMMER HOLIDAYS, EVERYONE!
WE MEET AGAIN ON...

Decide which hymns or songs you are going to sing and ask someone to play the piano for you. Give out the invitations in good time (see page 48). Ask everyone to bring a small photograph of their child. Produce an order of service (see example opposite).

Steady...

Read Mark 10:13–16; Proverbs 22:6

Go...

You're ready to help the children feel valued and most welcome in your church, even though they are small.

Let's begin!

Welcome

Begin the service by making everyone feel really welcome in the church. Some parents and carers may be anxious about their children making too much noise. Put them at ease at once by pointing out that a certain amount of noise is only to be expected. Encourage the adults to show the children any special features in the church after the service, such as a beautiful window, a cross and the font or baptistry.

For the adults

At some point in the service, explain that Jesus was indignant when his disciples tried to turn away parents with small children. He values children not just as future adults but as people in their own right with spiritual needs of their own. Jesus went on to explain that we need to develop a childlike trust in God, depending upon him just as a small child depends upon his or her parents, if we are to live the life God has planned for us.

Notices

Sing Happy Birthday to...

....

....

Suggested songs

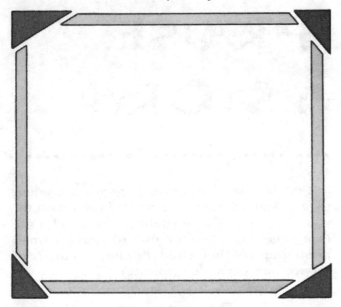

Jesus, we're here (*Feeling Good!*)
God bless you (*Feeling Good!*)
All things bright and beautiful (*Junior Praise*)
A wiggly waggly worm (*Junior Praise*)
Jesus' hands were kind hands (*Junior Praise*)
Praise him, praise him, all you little children (*Junior Praise*)
Thank you, Lord, for this fine day (*Junior Praise*)

Listen to *The Flight of the Bumble Bee* by Rimsky-Korsakov

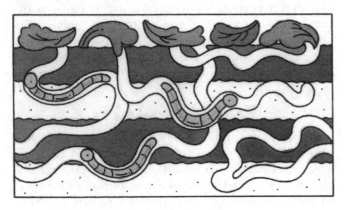

Nature notes

Go outside, if possible, to look for insects. Keep some in a jar on the nature table, but make sure that you also put in some damp soil or sand and some of the leaves from the plant on which you found them. Put on a lid that lets air in. Make a wormery to show how worms break up the earth and mix the layers. Talk about bees making honey and display a honeycomb.

Craft

Enlarge the picture of Jesus from page 46 and pin it to a board, ready for the children to add their photographs during the service.

(If the children are going to use the sheet individually, let them stick pictures of babies and children, from catalogues or magazines, around Jesus.)

Alternatively, let the adults write short prayers for their children on small pieces of coloured card to be stuck to the sheet.

In the classroom, let the children have fun making mini-beasts such as ladybirds, spiders, worms and snails from plasticine or card. Display them among the leaves, twigs and pine cones that you collected at the picnic.

Prayer

Ask _____ to read today's prayer, or print the prayer on the service sheet for everyone to say together.

Dear Father God, thank you for the Bible story we heard today, when Jesus said, 'Let the little children come to me!' We are here today as your children, big and small. Please bless us all, and help us to be a blessing to one another. Amen

Time for a story!

Rachel's mum was feeding the baby when Rachel said, 'Will you tell me a story?' Mum nodded.

'Just let me finish giving the baby his milk,' she said.

'Is it story time *now*?' Rachel asked a few moments later.

Mum smiled.

'I'll just wash the baby's face and put him in a clean nightie,' she said.

Rachel sighed. 'Babies take up a lot of time, don't they?'

'That's because they can't do much for themselves,' said Mum. 'They need their mums and dads to feed them and dress them and keep them safe.'

'But I need a story!' said Rachel. 'So *please* hurry up!'

Mum put the baby in his basket and sat down with Rachel.

'Once upon a time…' she began. But now someone was calling to them from the front door.

'Coo-ee! Is anyone at home?'

It was one of Mum's friends, carrying her baby.

'Oh no!' said Rachel. 'I'll never get my story now!'

Mum went to the door. She came back looking very excited.

'Quick!' she said. 'We're all going for a walk to the market place. Jesus is sitting under the big tree, talking to everyone in the village.'

Rachel felt rather cross. She didn't want to go out into the hot sunshine. She wanted to stay in the cool house and listen to a story.

The two mothers chattered all the way to the market place, their babies cradled in their arms. Rachel held on to her mum's dress and kicked at the stones on the dusty road. When they turned into the market place, Rachel opened her eyes wide. It was full of people.

'Look, Rachel! There's Jesus!' said Mum. 'Can you see him sitting in the middle of the crowd?'

Rachel looked and looked. At last, she saw a man who was smiling and moving his hands about as he spoke. But she couldn't hear what he was saying.

'Can we go a bit closer?' she asked.

Reproduced with permission from *Easy Ways to Seasonal Fun for the Very Young* published by BRF 2004 (1 84101 342 0)

They moved forward, stepping over the legs of people who were sitting on the ground.

'That's it, Rachel!' said Mum. 'If we can get close to Jesus, we'll ask him to bless you and the babies.'

'Bless us?' said Rachel in a loud voice. 'Whatever does "bless" mean?'

Some people looked round at her.

'Sssh! We can't hear what Jesus is saying!' they complained.

Mum bent down and whispered in Rachel's ear.

'We want Jesus to ask God to bring you lots of happiness,' she said.

At that moment, a man came to speak to Mum. 'Don't interrupt Jesus now!' he said crossly. 'Can't you see he's busy teaching the crowd?' Rachel looked up at Mum. She looked upset. Rachel leant against her and tried to hide in the folds of her dress.

Then something amazing happened. Jesus stood up, held out his arms and called, 'Let the little children come to me! I'm never too busy for children!'

Suddenly, people began to move out of their way. Hands pushed them gently towards Jesus.

'This way, dear!' said an old lady.

Rachel began to feel happy. She could feel a smile growing on her face. It felt as if the smile reached from one ear to the other. Mum was smiling broadly too. Then they were right next to Jesus. Rachel stared at his cloak. She saw his dusty toes peeping out from his sandals.

Jesus took the babies in his arms.

'May God bless you!' he said and the little ones opened their eyes and gazed up at him. Then Jesus knelt down so that he seemed to be no bigger than Rachel.

'And what can I do for you, Rachel?' he asked. Rachel looked at Mum and then back at Jesus.

'Would you tell me a story?' she asked shyly.

'A story!' said Jesus. 'Yes, of course! I'm very good at those!'

Sitting her on his knee, Jesus told Rachel her favourite story about Noah and all the animals in the ark. And Rachel felt very important sitting there with Jesus, listening to her own special story. And all the grown-ups enjoyed it too!

TODDLER PRAISE!

On: _____

In: _____

At: _____

Please do join us for this short and simple service especially designed for the children.

Please bring: _____

PICNIC TIME!

Place: _____

On: _____

At: _____

We provide: _____

Please bring: _____

RSVP by: _____

To: _____

WE WOULD LOVE TO SEE YOU!

Autumn

HARVEST: WHAT'S IN THE BASKET?

Introduction

This is an appropriate session to use in September, when new children come into your group or class, because it teaches them who God is (the creator) and what he is like (his generosity) with reference to the natural world around them.

Ready...

Pack the story basket with different types of fruit, vegetables and breads, making sure that there is a good variety of colours, shapes, sizes and textures, and some unusual ones, too. Take along a fruit bowl, vegetable rack and bread bin.

Steady...

Read Genesis 1:1—2:4; Deuteronomy 26:1–4; Psalm 8; Psalm 104

Go...

You're ready to inspire the children with delight at the sheer abundance and diversity of creation and to encourage them to share good gifts with others.

Let's begin!

Welcome

Welcome everyone! Especially…

For the adults

The creation story is not intended to tell us *how* the universe was created—scientists are still not certain about that today. The important point made by the writer of these poetic verses is that our world did not happen by accident but rather at the will of God. He has made abundant provision for all his creatures. But by making us in his own image, he has placed a special responsibility upon us to use the world's resources in a fair manner.

If we can help children to discover a sense of joy in nature, it is something that will benefit them all their lives.

Notices

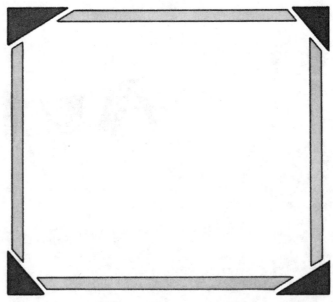

Sing Happy Birthday to...

The story basket

Ask the children if they ever help with the shopping. Tell them that Teddy has been helping Mrs Bear. His basket is very heavy because it is full of food. Look! There are all sorts of fruit and vegetables and breads. Shall we help Teddy put all the shopping away in the right place?

Bring out the items one by one. See if the children can identify them and put them into the fruit bowl, vegetable rack or bread bin. Encourage them to feel the textures, look at the shapes and colours and smell the items. Which are their favourite foods? Praise the children when everything has been neatly stored away. Teddy's basket is light now because it is empty and ready to fill again next time he goes shopping. Teddy thanks the children for helping him.

> **And let's say 'thank you, God' for making us so many different kinds of food to enjoy!**

Suggested songs

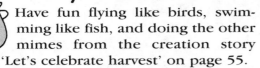

Pat-a-cake, pat-a-cake, baker's man
The sun has got his hat on
Hey diddle diddle, the cat and the fiddle
I like eating (*Feeling Good!*)
Think of a world without any flowers (*Junior Praise*)
Someone's brought a loaf of bread (*Junior Praise*)
Open our eyes, Lord (*Songs of Fellowship*)

Play acting

Have fun flying like birds, swimming like fish, and doing the other mimes from the creation story 'Let's celebrate harvest' on page 55.

If you would like a 'sharing' activity, ask some children with baskets to stand in the middle of a circle of seated children. Adapt the song 'There's a hole in my bucket' so that the children sing:

Verse 1: *Say what's in your basket, dear Sophie, dear Sophie…* (and so on). *Say what!*

Verse 2: *There are cakes in my basket, dear children…* (and so on). *Some cakes!*

Verse 3: *Then share them, dear Sophie…* (and so on). *Share them!*

Everyone should have one of each item on their plate at the end of the song.

Nature notes

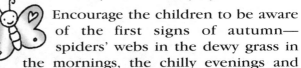

Encourage the children to be aware of the first signs of autumn— spiders' webs in the dewy grass in the mornings, the chilly evenings and the harvest moon hanging low and golden. Perhaps you could walk to some allotments. Explain that we have to pick fruit and vegetables and store them in a shed or garage before the first frosts can get at them. Dry big sunflower heads and keep them for the class bird table.

Talk about hibernating animals, such as hedgehogs and bats, that are fattening themselves up in readiness for the winter. Can the children spot any squirrels? They are hiding nuts now in various places to find during a mild midwinter spell.

You could plant bulbs in bowls for a classroom display at Christmas.

Craft

You could show the children pictures of famous still-life paintings in books or on postcards.

Let the children colour the circle of fruit on the craft page (page 58) before they glue it on to their basket. Provide tiny pieces of screwed-up coloured tissue paper for them to stick in the spaces around the fruit. Glue a small bow to the handle.

Help the children to make the collages for the harvest celebration, as indicated in the script (pages 55–56).

Prayer

Ask _____ to read today's prayer.

Each, peach, pear, plum,
I spy the golden sun.
The golden sun shines on my tree,
I spy apples for my tea.
My tea's all gone—it's bedtime soon,
I spy the harvest moon.
The harvest moon shines on the stair,
Let's say a harvest prayer!
Each, peach, pear, plum,
Thank you, God, for harvest fun! Amen

Who made the sun?

NB: This is an interactive story. Encourage the children to repeat the words written in bold when you hold up the appropriate drawing, photocopied and cut out from the templates on page 52.

One afternoon, Mrs Bear went to wake Teddy from his afternoon nap. 'Let there be light!' said Mrs Bear as she opened his bedroom curtains. The sunshine streamed into Teddy's bedroom. It made Mrs Bear sneeze.

'Uh - uh - uh pchooooo!'

'Bless you!' said Teddy, sitting up in bed. 'Who made the sun?'

'God did,' said Mrs Bear. **'God made the sun.'**

'Where *is* God?' asked Teddy. 'Can I see him?'

'God is everywhere,' explained Mrs Bear. 'You can't see him. But if you go out into the garden, you can see all the beautiful things that he has made.'

Teddy couldn't wait to go out into the garden. The first thing that he saw was **the old sycamore tree**. Teddy scrambled up on to a strong branch. Then he looked up. The tree reached up and up until it seemed to touch the bright blue sky. 'This tree must have been growing here for a very long time,' thought Teddy.

Then he heard a thin, piping song. Something fluttered its feathery wings in the branches above his head. It was a bird.

'Hello, Mr Blackbird!' said Teddy. 'I've heard you singing to me at bedtime and when I wake up in the morning.'

Suddenly, the blackbird made a different sound.

'Bink, bink!' he called, as if to say, 'Look, look! Look who's coming!'

Teddy stared down into the garden. Something was stalking through the long grass like a lion in the jungle. But **it was only Teddy's cat**. Teddy jumped down to stroke him and the cat rubbed itself all round Teddy's legs.

'Hello, Pussy Willow!' said Teddy. 'What a good friend you are!'

Teddy and Pussy Willow wandered down the garden and

found a rosy apple lying under the apple tree. Teddy picked it up.

'This apple smells delicious,' exclaimed Teddy. 'Let's go indoors and ask Mummy to wash it for our tea.'

'Did you have a lovely time in the garden?' asked Mrs Bear.

'Yes!' answered Teddy. 'I didn't see God, but I could feel his warm sunshine all over my furry face!'

'And **I can see his beautiful moon!**' said Mrs Bear as she closed the curtains. 'That means it must be nearly bedtime!'

Let's celebrate harvest!

Play a harvest hymn or 'Autumn' from the *Four Seasons* by Vivaldi as the children place their harvest gifts on the table.

Leader: Just look at our harvest table! It's overflowing with harvest gifts. You've all been working very hard to fill your baskets and boxes and to make them look so beautiful! Let's see what's in some of the baskets. A tin of beans… a loaf of bread… a box of tea… *(and so on)*.

Song

Someone's brought a loaf of bread (*Junior Praise*)

Leader: Thank you very much, everyone, for all your hard work. But do you know who made all these wonderful things for us? It was God! He worked very hard to make our world and to fill it up with all kinds of fruit and flowers and vegetables. The story of how God made the world is called the story of creation. Some of you are going to help me tell that story.

In the beginning, there was nothing. *(Show empty hands.)*
    So God made the heavens and the earth.
        'Let there be light!' said God.
        And light appeared!

(Turn over the 'h' to reveal a glittery picture.)

'That's good!' said God. 'That's very good!'

God made the land. But there was nothing growing on it.
    'Let all kinds of plants grow on the earth!' said God.
    And they did!

(Turn over the 'a' to reveal a plant collage, or mime growing tall.)

'That's good!' said God. 'That's very good!'

God made the sky. But there was nothing shining in it!

'Let there be lights in the sky!' said God. And there were!

(Turn over the 'r' to reveal planets and stars, or wiggle fingers like shining stars.)

Bright suns and moons and stars filled the sky!

'That's good!' said God. 'That's very good!'

God made the sea. But there was nothing swimming in it!

'Let the sea be filled with all sorts of sea creatures!' said God.

And it was!

(Turn over the 'v' to reveal a fish collage, or mime swimming.)

There were *(as appropriate)* fish and crabs and dolphins and sea-horses all swimming through the water!

'That's good!' said God. 'That's very good!'

God made the air. But there was nothing flying through it.

'Let there be birds!' said God.

And there were!

(Turn over the 'e' to reveal a bird collage, or mime flying.)

The air was filled with birds!

'That's good!' said God. 'That's very good.'

God made the jungle. He made forests, fields and gardens. But there was nothing galloping, trotting, hopping or crawling through it.

'Let there be animals!' said God.

And there were!

(Turn over the 's' to reveal an animal collage, or mime different animal movements.)

There were big animals and small animals. There were wild animals and friendly pets.

'That's good!' said God. 'That's very good!'

So, God made the world. But there was no one to look after it.

'Let there be boys and girls!' said God.

And there were!

(Turn over the 't' to reveal a collage of children, or mime gardening.)

The world was filled with people sowing seeds and watering their plants and gathering in the harvest fruit and vegetables.

'That's good!' said God. 'That's very good!'

And God was so pleased with what he had made that he stopped for a rest!

God is still making lots of good things for us today. But he wants us to help him to share these good gifts with each other so that no one will have empty hands. Let's sing a song that's all about sharing...

Song

Sing to the tune of 'In and out the windows'.

Gather in the harvest,
Gather in the harvest,
Gather in the harvest,
As we have done before.

Share it with your neighbour,
Share it with your neighbour,
Share it with your neighbour,
For there is plenty more.

Then, *no one will be hungry,*
No one will be hungry,
No one will be hungry,
As they have been before.

Prayer

Ask _____ to read today's prayer.

Dear God, thank you for making our world, and for filling it up with so many good things. Please help us to look after your world, and to share all the good things we have with other people. Amen

A harvest basket for you to make!

Colour the circle of fruit and glue it on to the basket. Decorate with tiny pieces of screwed-up coloured tissue paper and glue a small bow to the handle.

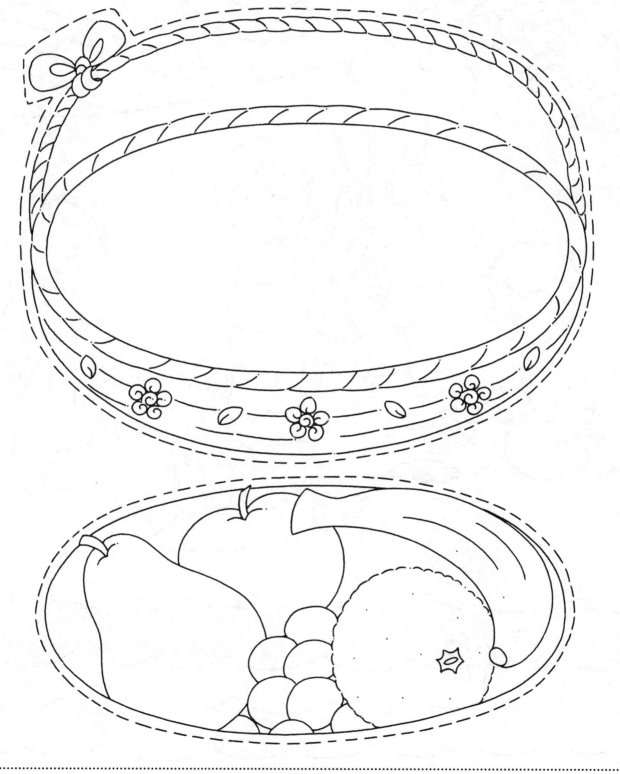

ALL SAINTS' DAY: PUT ON THE LIGHTS!

Introduction

All Saints' Day on 1 November is the day on which we remember Christians who have lived particularly good and holy lives. The word 'saint' means someone who has dedicated themselves to the service of God. Since Christians try to live their lives doing God's will, the word could be applied to all Christians.

In this session, the children think about different light sources and the way they keep us safe, before they listen to the story of Florence Nightingale, the lady with the lamp.

Ready...

Pack the story basket with:
- some fluorescent or white clothing for Teddy
- a torch
- some silver stars and a moon
- a table lamp

Steady...

Read John 8:12; Ephesians 5:1–20; Philippians 2:12–18

Go...

You're ready to inspire the children with the thought that they can really make a difference to our world by 'shining their lights'!

★ ★ ★

Let's begin!

Welcome

Welcome everyone! Especially…

For the adults

Sometimes it may seem as if our small acts of kindness are mere drops in the ocean. But they may make a world of difference to the person we have helped. They are rather like the collection boxes for small coins in some shops: the total amounts to an incredible sum.

Notices

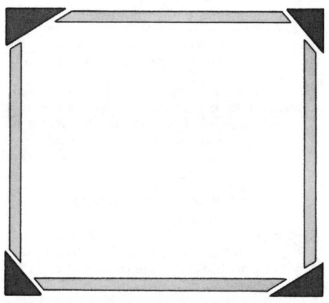

Sing Happy Birthday to...

The story basket

Tell the children that the weather can sometimes be foggy in November. Make up a story about Teddy walking to school on a foggy morning. One November morning, Teddy looks out of his front door and has a big surprise.

'What's happened to the world?' asks Teddy. 'I can't see the house across the road. I can't see the front gate. I can't even see the tip of my nose.' Mrs Bear explains to Teddy that they must wear something very bright in the fog so that they will be sure to show up as they walk along the pavement.

(Dress Teddy in the fluorescent or white clothing and bring out the torch.) Now Teddy can see where he is going and the people driving their cars can see him too. On the way home, it is getting dark and gloomy, but Teddy cheers up when he sees the moon and the stars. Mrs Bear has even put a lamp in the window to welcome them when they get home.

> **Teddy asks if God can see him when it is foggy. God can always see us, however dark and gloomy it is!**

Suggested songs

Twinkle, twinkle, little star
Candle time (*Feeling Good!*)
This little light of mine (*Junior Praise*)
Jesus bids us shine (*Junior Praise*)

Play acting

Talk to the children about lights that guide us and keep us safe—for example, cat's eyes, lighthouses, bicycle lamps, pedestrian crossing lights. Play 'Traffic-lights' with the children.

- Green means walk about.
- Red means stop.
- Amber means get ready to go, or slow down.

Explain that everyone is special and has something that they can do well. All join hands and circle as you sing the chorus. Then each child demonstrates something, or shows a good piece of work in the centre of the circle, before you join hands ready to circle again.

Here we go Looby Loo,
Here we go Looby Light,
Here we go Looby Loo,
All on a Saturday night!

Peter can hop/skip/jump/draw like this,
Peter can hop like that,
Peter can hop like this,
So give him a great big clap! (CLAP CLAP)

Nature notes

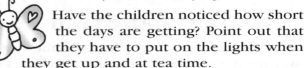

Have the children noticed how short the days are getting? Point out that they have to put on the lights when they get up and at tea time.

You might like to provide a bird table so that the children can feed and watch the resident birds during the winter months. Point out the robin with his red breast—the young robins are getting their colours now. Explain how they use a flash of their red breasts to defend their territory from other birds. You could also talk about animals that hibernate, such as hedgehogs, bats, badgers and snakes. Bring in a snail to look at the tough door it grows to close off its shell.

Bring in some old man's beard (wild clematis), some silvery honesty seed pods that resemble the moon (*Lunaria biennis*) or some Chinese lanterns (*Physalis alkekengi*).

Craft

Show the children a picture of Holman Hunt's famous painting *The Light of the World*, pointing out the lantern.

Let the children light the lantern on the craft sheet on page 65 by pasting the candle into the lantern. Decorate the top with star stickers and hang the lantern using colourful wool.

Paint pictures or make models of lights that guide us.

Make traffic-light biscuits by icing some rectangular biscuits and adding red, orange and green Smarties.

Prayer

Ask _____ to read today's prayer.

Dear God, thank you for torches and lamps that light up the pavement and show us where to walk. Thank you for the gift of light God has made for our world that we see in the sun, the moon and the stars. Amen

All Saints' Day celebration

(Some children come out to the front to show their models or paintings of lights.)

Leader: Now we're going to sing a song about some lights that help us in the dark.

Song

Sing to the tune of 'The wise man built his house upon the rock'.

The lighthouse says, 'Be careful of the rocks!' (x 3) (flash torches)
And the boats sail safely round.

The runway lights say, 'This is where to land!' (x 3) (flash two lines of torches)
And the planes fly safely down.

The traffic-lights say, 'Cars must stop and go!' (x 3)
And the cars drive safely round.

The torch light says, 'I'll show you where to walk!' (x 3) (walk with torches)
And it keeps me safe and sound.

Leader: There are some people I know who are so kind and cheerful and helpful that they seem to glow like lights. They make the world a much brighter place. Do you know anyone like that? On 1 November, All Saints' Day, we remember all the people who have spent their lives helping others. We call them 'saints'. This is the story of just one of those people who shone like a light.

A team member reads the story of Florence Nightingale...

Close the curtains and let the children have a torchlight procession into the hall or show them to their places with torches. You could put up some fairy lights and play 'Sing a rainbow' (*Apusskidu*) as they come in. Or you could play Handel's Fireworks Music.

Leader: How lovely to see all those torches! I wonder how dark it would be without all your torches shining. Let's see! ... Oh, dear! Very gloomy! Would someone put on the hall lights, please? Ah, that's much better. Lights are very helpful things, aren't they? They cheer us up on dark November days and they guide us and keep us safe. How many lights can you think of that save us from danger?

Florence Nightingale: the lady with the lamp

There was once a young lady called Florence Nightingale. *(Someone could act the part or show a Victorian doll.)* She was born when Queen Victoria was on the throne, so she would have worn Victorian clothes like these.

Florence knew what she wanted to be when she grew up. She wanted to be a nurse and to look after people who weren't very well in hospital. In those days, hospitals were very dirty places. So Florence's mum and dad said, 'You can't go to work in a hospital. A lovely young lady like you? Oh no! You must stay at home and play the piano.' *(All mime playing the piano.)*

But Florence knew that God wanted her to help other people. So, whenever she was on her own, Florence read a lot of books about making people better. *(All mime reading.)*

When she was older, Florence packed her suitcase and went travelling. *(Florence walks around with her case.)* She helped at hospitals in the countries that she visited.

Then a terrible war broke out. It was called the Crimean War. Many, many soldiers were hurt in the fighting. They were taken to a hospital in a country called Turkey. *(Boys sit on chairs around Florence.)*

But there weren't enough doctors to look after the soldiers. There weren't enough bandages or medicines. Imagine being in bed with no one to make you well again!

Florence Nightingale packed her bag again and set off to find that hospital. She took some friends with her to help her with the work. *(Girls stand behind the chairs.)* And do you know what the first thing was that they did? They rolled up their sleeves and they scrubbed that hospital from top to bottom. *(All mime scrubbing.)* Then they washed the sheets and pyjamas. *(All mime washing.)* And they sewed the buttons back on to them too. *(All mime sewing.)*

Florence and her nurses bandaged the wounded soldiers, and made them feel much more cheerful. At night time, Florence used to walk around the beds with her lamp to make sure that the soldiers had everything they needed. The soldiers made up a special name for Florence. They called her 'the Lady with the Lamp'!

When Florence came home again, she started a school for girls to learn how to be good nurses. She also made sure that hospitals were clean and safe places.

Leader: I'm sure those soldiers felt much happier when Florence came to look after them. I wonder what *you* could do to cheer up another person? Perhaps you could make a 'get well' card for someone you know who isn't very well. Perhaps you could make friends with someone new. It might not seem very much *(switch on one torch)* but if everyone did something kind, we could brighten up the whole world! Let's all switch our torches on again… and we're going to sing:

Song

This little light of mine

Prayer

Ask _____ to read today's prayer.

Dear God, thank you for people who spend their lives being kind and helpful to others. Please help us to brighten up your world by being kind and helpful too. Amen

Shine like a star
lighting up the sky!

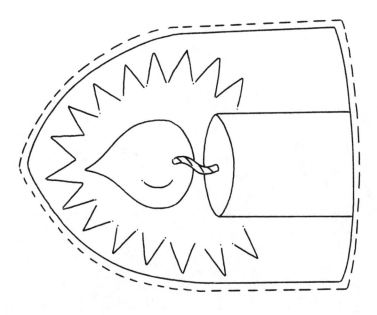

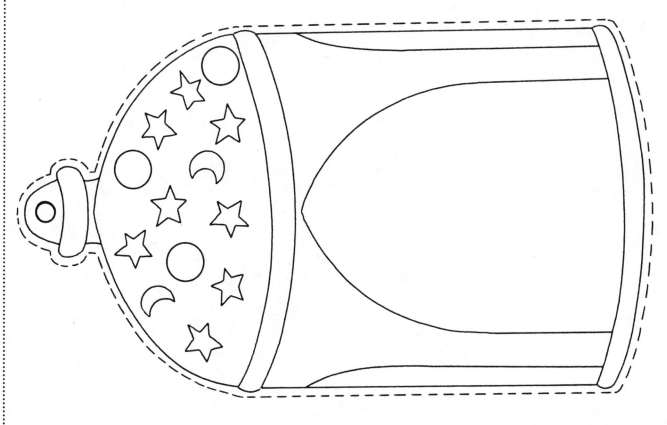

Reproduced with permission from *Easy Ways to Seasonal Fun for the Very Young* published by BRF 2004 (1 84101 342 0)

Winter

ADVENT: LET'S GET READY TO WELCOME JESUS!

Introduction

In this session, an angel Christmas tree decoration leads into the Bible story of the angel Gabriel telling Mary that she will be the mother of Jesus. A short mimed presentation of the legend of the first Christmas tree underlines the idea of welcoming Jesus into our homes or schools at this exciting time of year.

Ready...

Pack the story basket with a selection of Christmas and Christmas tree decorations such as tinsel, paper chains, baubles, stars, a robin and so on, but definitely include an angel. Take along a small Christmas tree or a wintry branch to decorate, and wind some tinsel round Teddy's head.

Steady...

Read Luke 1:26–38

Go...

You're ready to show that all the 'busyness' in the run-up to Christmas is in preparation for the coming of Jesus.

★ ★ ★

Let's begin!

Welcome

Welcome everyone! Especially…

For the adults

The danger for adults is that we forget what Christmas is all about in the stress we cause ourselves, trying to give our families 'the perfect Christmas'. By simplifying the food and presents (perhaps with an agreed price limit) we could concentrate on providing a warm and welcoming atmosphere—far more important than elaborate gifts and cuisine.

Notices

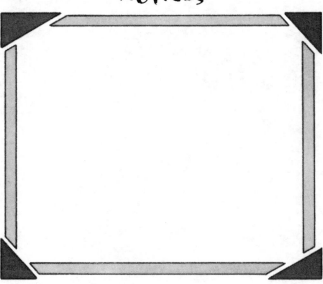

Sing Happy Birthday to...

::

The story basket

Point out to the children that Teddy is wearing something very sparkly. 'You've got tinsel round your head, Teddy! Why are you wearing that?' *(He whispers in your ear.)* Teddy says that he is getting ready for Christmas. He wants to make the classroom look beautiful. That's why he has brought along his basket of Christmas decorations from the attic. Let's have a look at them.

Bring out the decorations one by one and comment on the colours and the textures. Let the children hang the tree decorations and finish by putting the angel on the top of the tree. Point out her wings and her halo and explain that angels bring messages from God. Teddy thinks the tree looks lovely. What fun it is getting ready for Christmas!

Teddy asks why we are so busy decorating at Christmas…

> **It's because we are getting ready to welcome Jesus, the very special baby who was born at Christmas.**

Suggested songs

Little Jack Horner
You are welcome (*Feeling Good!*)
The angels (*Feeling Good!*)
O Christmas tree, O Christmas tree
(*Carol, gaily carol*)

Play acting

Ask the children whether anyone special ever comes to visit their home. Perhaps it's a grandparent, an aunt or uncle or a favourite cousin. Do they get excited about the visit? Why is that person so special to them? What do they do to get ready? Mime these things—for example, making up a bed, icing a cake, dusting the house. You could adapt 'Here we go round the mulberry bush', so that you sing, 'This is the way we pick some flowers/clean the bath/hang balloons' and so on. End by imagining that the person has arrived and is standing at the front door, ringing or knocking. The children run to open the front door and welcome their visitor.

Nature notes

See if the children can spot some evergreen trees, and contrast them with the bare branches of the deciduous trees. Let them examine pine cones and pine needles. You may like to spray some cones with gold or silver for Christmas decorations.

Make a Christmas tree for the birds by hanging bits of coconut, bacon rind, string bags of peanuts, seeds and biscuits on a small fir tree outside. Don't forget to put plenty of food and water on your bird table.

Craft

Show the children any pictures that you can find (especially from classical art) of the angel Gabriel visiting Mary. Point out the different ways in which the angel is portrayed. What do they think an angel would look like? What do they think he is saying to Mary?

Make star Christmas tree decorations for the story of the little fir tree on page 73, by cutting star shapes out of silver card and adding glitter and a ribbon. There is a star template for you to copy on page 95.

Make the angel on the craft sheet on page 75. Cut out the angel and wings and let the children decorate them. Fold the angel into a cone shape and glue the edges together. Glue the wings into position. Add a loop of ribbon and hang the angel on a Christmas tree or branch.

Prayer

Ask _____ to read today's prayer.

Dear God,
Thank you for angels to hang on the tree.
Thank you for tinsel, as bright as could be.
Oh help us remember what all this is for—
To welcome the baby who slept in the straw.
You are welcome, baby Jesus! Amen

The angel visitor

All sorts of visitors come to our homes every day. When you hear someone knocking at the door or ringing the bell, do you run to see who is there?

Sometimes a friend has come to play. Or perhaps a babysitter has come to look after you for a little while. Sometimes it's the postman with a parcel that won't fit through the letterbox. But how would you feel if an angel came to visit you? I wonder what you would do! I wonder what you would say!

That's just what happened to a girl called Mary. One day, when she wasn't expecting anyone to call, an angel came to visit her. The angel's name was Gabriel and he brought Mary a message from God.

'Hello, Mary! Greetings!' said the angel politely. 'God has sent me to tell you some news!'

Mary looked very worried, so the angel said, 'Don't be afraid, Mary. God is very pleased with you. He wants you to have a baby—a very special baby boy. The baby's name will be Jesus and he will grow up to be the most important king in the world. He will be a king for ever!'

'But how will all of this happen?' asked Mary, feeling very puzzled. The angel smiled kindly. 'God will take care of everything,' he said. 'You see, the baby boy will be God's very own Son. Don't forget, God can do anything!'

Then Mary said, 'I love God very much and I will do whatever he asks. How lucky I am that I will be the mother of Jesus.'

And as Mary was thinking about all the things she would do to get ready for the baby, the angel flew on his way. I wonder what Mary was planning to do. Can you guess?

Welcome, baby Jesus! Welcome!

Props

You will need:

★ An Advent calendar showing a nativity scene
★ A Christmas tree angel
★ A small lantern
★ A baby doll
★ Silver stars *(see craft activity)*
★ Musical triangles
★ A toy lamb
★ A small fir tree in a tub

Cast

Mary
Joseph
An angel
Innkeeper
Shepherds
Nativity children
The innkeeper's animals

Play a Christmas carol such as 'The holly and the ivy' or 'Deck the hall with boughs of holly' as the children come in.

Leader: Welcome to our Advent assembly/ concert, everyone! The weeks before Christmas are very exciting, aren't they? I wonder what you've all been doing to get ready? Perhaps you've been opening the windows on your Advent calendars. *(Show a calendar with a nativity scene on it.)* There's a window to open every day until Christmas Day—the day when Jesus was born.

Perhaps you've been lighting an Advent candle? Or perhaps you've been decorating a Christmas tree with an angel on the top? *(Show an angel.)* It was an angel who told Mary that she was going to have a very special baby called Jesus. Let's sing an Advent song—a song about the baby who is coming at Christmas.

Song

Sing to the tune of *Frère Jacques*:

Someone's coming,
Someone's coming,
A baby boy!
A baby boy!
Listen to the angel,
Listen to the angel
Tell of joy,
Tell of joy!

Leader: Our story today is all about a little fir tree who really wanted to welcome baby Jesus into the world. Can you see the tree? It's quite difficult to spot because it doesn't have any lights or decorations in its branches. In fact, its branches are very bare—and very spiky!

Well, an old legend says that this tree grew in the very barn in Bethlehem where Jesus was born. *(Gesture to nativity children.)* The barn belonged to an innkeeper—can you see him holding up his lantern? And there's Mary, the baby's mother *(she waves)* and Joseph *(he waves)* and all the innkeeper's animals gathered round the manger. *(They wave or make the appropriate animal noise.)* They must have been very surprised to find a baby lying in their feed box! Can you show us your baby, Mary? *(She holds up the baby doll.)*

Up above the barn roof, many stars twinkled in the night sky. *(Children hold up the silver stars they have made, while others play triangles.)* But *inside* the stable, it was dark and very cold…

Song

The north wind doth blow,
And we shall have snow,
And what will the baby do then,
poor thing?
Shut the barn door,
And lay him in straw,
For there is no room at the inn,
poor thing!

Leader: The little fir tree sighed. 'What a wretched place for a baby to be born!' he exclaimed. 'How I wish that my branches were decorated with bright lights to welcome him!'

At that moment, the barn door opened and a cold draught made the little tree shiver. Some shepherds from the hillside hurried inside, bringing a newborn lamb for the baby. *(Shepherds tiptoe to kneel at the manger.)*

'A bright and shining angel told us where to find Jesus,' said a shepherd boy. 'So we ran here as quickly as we could.'

'Oh, if only *I* had legs to run about on like those shepherds,' cried the fir tree. 'Why, I would run all over the place looking for something to decorate this gloomy old barn!'

Song

Sing to the tune of 'I had a little nut tree'.

I had a little fir tree,
Nothing would it bear
But a bumpy fir cone
In its spiky hair;
A baby king called Jesus
Came to visit me,
And lay beneath the boughs
of my little fir tree;
I'd skip over water and dance over sea,
To decorate the boughs
of my little fir tree!

Leader: The little fir tree felt so sad that he hung his head, and a few pine-needle tears fell on to the stable floor. The bright and shining angel was on her way back to heaven when she heard the little fir tree crying. *(An angel comes to stand before the scene, arm raised.)*

'Fear not!' she said. 'I will ask the stars to come down and nestle in your branches. You will be the very first Christmas tree! Come along, stars! Decorate this Christmas tree!'

At once, the stars came shooting out of the sky and settled in the fir tree's spiky branches. *(The 'stars' hang their star shapes on the tree while the 'triangles' play.)*

How that barn glowed in the soft starlight! 'Thank you!' exclaimed the Christmas tree. 'Look! The baby is gazing at the lights in my branches.' *(Mary holds up the baby doll.)*

'You have welcomed a great king into the world,' said the angel. 'For this baby is Jesus, the Son of God.'

All: Welcome, baby Jesus! Welcome!

Leader: What a kind little fir tree! He really wanted to give Jesus a warm welcome into his home, even though it was just a chilly barn. But how can *we* welcome Jesus at Christmas time? We can welcome him just by remembering what Christmas is all about. It's all about the coming of Jesus. And that's what 'Advent' means—it means 'coming'.

Prayer

Ask _____ to read today's prayer.

Dear God, thank you for this exciting time of year. Please show us what we can do to help our mums and dads and our teachers to get ready for Christmas. Help us to be kind and welcoming to anyone who comes to stay with us in the holidays. And please don't let us forget about Jesus in all our excitement. Amen

Make an angel
to hang on your tree!

Reproduced with permission from *Easy Ways to Seasonal Fun for the Very Young* published by BRF 2004 (1 84101 342 0)

CHRISTMAS: B IS FOR BABY!

Introduction

In this session, the children think about the arrival of a new baby, before listening to the nativity story. A simple mimed play helps them to understand that Jesus was born in a humble stable.

Ready...

Pack the story basket with:
- Baby items that all begin with the letter B (such as bib, bootees, bottle, baby brush and blue balloons)
- A big letter B written on white card
- A tiny teddy (Little Ted) wrapped up in a blanket, perhaps in a baby basket
- A birth announcement card

Steady...

Read Luke 2:1–20

Go...

You're ready to inspire the children with excitement at the arrival of a new baby. Be sensitive to anyone who might be feeling put out by the arrival of a new baby at home. Help them to feel special, perhaps by inviting the parent and the baby into the classroom.

★ ★ ★

Let's begin!

Welcome

Welcome everyone! Especially...

For the adults

Christmas can be a particularly difficult time when life is hard. Yet we have romanticized the nativity story, ignoring the fact that Mary gave birth in a chilly, dirty stable, far from home, and that Jesus would have cried with the cold like any other baby. We can find comfort in the knowledge that 'God is with us' through the birth of his Son, Jesus. He understands our problems because he experienced all the hardships of human life himself.

Notices

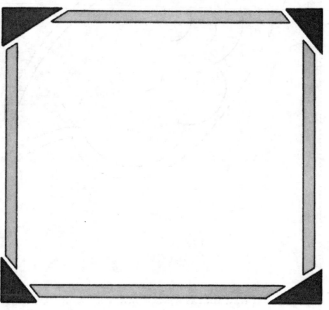

Sing Happy Birthday to...

```
..........................................
.                                        .
.                                        .
.                                        .
..........................................
```

The story basket

Tie the blue balloons where the children can see them but where there is no danger of them popping.

Say, 'Look, everyone! Teddy has tied some balloons to his front door. I wonder why. Perhaps it's Teddy's birthday. Is it your birthday, Teddy?' *(He shakes his head.)* 'No! Then why…?' *(Teddy whispers in your ear.)* 'How lovely! Teddy's mummy has just had a baby—a little brother for Teddy. Teddy is waiting for Mrs Bear to bring him home from the hospital.'

Teddy shows the children all the things that he has been getting ready for the baby. They all begin with… *(show the card)* B!

Bring out the items and see if the children can name them and tell you what they are for. Teddy is very excited now because his mummy should be here with his baby brother at any minute. Say, 'Let's listen for a knock at the door. Knock, knock! Who's there? It's Teddy's baby brother, Little Ted!' *(Bring out the small teddy.)* 'Isn't he lovely? Let's all say "well done" to Teddy for having such a lovely baby brother! Give him a clap. Now Teddy has a very important job to do, helping to look after the baby.'

> **And let's say 'Thank you, God' for all the excitement of a new baby.**

Suggested songs

Rock-a-bye baby
Pat-a-cake, pat-a-cake, baker's man
Lullaby Jesus *(Feeling Good!)*
Christmas is a happy time *(Feeling Good!)*
A baby was born *(Feeling Good!)*
Long ago there was born *(Junior Praise)* (The music is adapted from the famous Brahms *Lullaby*)

Play 'Winter' from the *Four Seasons* by Vivaldi

Play acting

With the children all sitting in a circle, explain that babies can't do very much for themselves. They need mums or dads or even big brothers or sisters to look after them. Ask the children to mime putting a bib on the baby, feeding him with a bottle, gently brushing his hair, putting his bootees on and then rocking him to sleep. Explain what a lullaby is and practise singing one very softly.

Nature notes

Cheer up the nature table with a poinsettia (and give it as a gift to someone who helps with the play on page 80) or a vase of rose-hips.

If snow has fallen, take the children out to look for bird and animal footprints. Draw and label some for the nature table. Talk to the children about animal homes: horse/stable; pig/sty; dog/kennel; cow/barn; rabbit/hutch; doves/dovecote and so on. Explain how creatures with fur grow thicker coats to keep them warm, while we have to wear woollen jumpers and coats.

Craft

Look at nativity scenes on Christmas cards, pointing out the stable, the manger and the animals. Make a Christmas card by folding coloured card in half and pasting the stable from the bottom half of the craft sheet (page 82) on to the front. When the children have decorated it, let them cut out the doors from the top half of the craft sheet and paste them over the stable scene. Alternatively, use the pictures to make an invitation to the play.

Prayer

Ask _____ to read today's prayer.

Dear God, thank you for baby Jesus, who was born in a stable with all the animals at Christmas time. Thank you that you sent him to be our brother. Amen

B is for baby!

Most babies are born in a hospital or at home in a warm bedroom. But baby Jesus was born in a very unusual place, and this is how it happened.

One day, Mary could feel the baby inside her tummy stretching its arms and kicking its little legs. 'The baby will be born soon!' said Mary to Joseph. 'Oh, won't it be exciting to have a new baby in the house!'

But Joseph had something to tell Mary.

'Mary,' he said. 'I'm afraid we must go all the way to Bethlehem to pay our taxes.'

'Oh no!' exclaimed Mary. 'But what will happen if the baby is born while we are away?'

'Don't worry!' said Joseph. 'There are lots of hotels and inns in Bethlehem. We'll find somewhere comfortable to stay.'

Mary rode to Bethlehem on a little donkey. She remembered to pack some baby clothes in the donkey's baskets—just in case! When at last they arrived in Bethlehem, Mary couldn't wait to lie down in a warm bed. Joseph knocked on the door of an inn. Knock, knock! Who's there?

'It's Mary and Joseph, looking for a room for the night.'

'Sorry. We're full up!' said the innkeeper. 'Try next door!'

Mary and Joseph did try next door. They tried *everywhere*. But all the inns were full. A light shone out from under the door of a stable. Joseph knocked once more. Knock, knock!

'Who's there?' said the innkeeper, who was saying 'goodnight' to his animals.

'It's Mary and Joseph, looking for somewhere—*anywhere*—to sleep for the night. Mary's baby might be born tonight!'

The innkeeper smiled and his eyes twinkled kindly.

'Do come in!' he said. 'I'll fetch some fresh straw to make you a bed.'

And that's how it happened that Jesus was born in a stable, among all the animals. Mary laid him in the manger, which was really the animals' feed box. God hung a bright star in the sky. And his angels sang a beautiful song to tell the good news to some shepherds on the hillside. They came running to see the baby in the manger— well, wouldn't you?

Knock, knock!
Who's there?

Twinkle, twinkle little star...

Props

You will need:
★ A manger containing hay
★ A baby doll

Cast

Innkeeper
Two mice
Two owls
Two kittens
Two doves
Two lambs
Mary
Joseph
Shepherds
Angels

Play a carol such as 'In the bleak midwinter', or 'For unto us a child is born' from Handel's *Messiah*.

Leader: Here is the kind innkeeper who lives in Bethlehem. When he smiles, his eyes *twinkle, twinkle* like the stars in the night sky.

Sing the song 'Twinkle, twinkle, little star'.

Leader: One starry night, many visitors come to Bethlehem. They *knock, knock* upon the innkeeper's door.
All: Knock, knock!
Leader: 'Do come in!' he says. And soon the inn is full.

After supper, the innkeeper goes round to the stable to put his animals to bed for the night. He hangs his lantern on the old beam. Then he fills the manger with fresh hay.

'Come along, come along!' he calls to the animals.

Soon the stable is *almost* full. But not quite! For just as the

	innkeeper is saying 'goodnight'…
Mice:	Squeak, squeak!
All:	Who's there?
Leader:	Why, it's two little mice looking for a mouse hole for the night. Do come in!
Owls:	Tu-whit, tu-whoo!
All:	Who's there?
Leader:	Why, it's two little owls looking for an old beam to settle down upon for the night. Do come in!
Kittens:	Meow, meow!
All:	Who's there?
Leader:	Why, it's two little kittens looking for a pile of straw to curl up in for the night. Do come in!
	Then, as the innkeeper walks towards the door…
Mary and Joseph:	Knock, knock!
All:	Who's there?
Leader:	Why, it's Mary and Joseph looking for somewhere—*anywhere*—to stay for the night. Mary's baby will be born tonight. Do come in!
	Much later on, the animals are woken by a strange sound that seems to come from the manger.
All:	Gurgle, gurgle, snuffle, snuffle, waaa, waaa, WAAA!

Leader:	'Who's there?' call the owls.
Owls:	Whoo, whoo?
Leader:	Why! It's baby Jesus—the King of kings—lying in the manger! The doves sing him a lullaby.
Doves:	Coo, coo! Coo, coo!

Sing the song 'Away in a manger'

Leader:	'That's quite enough excitement for one night!' says the innkeeper. 'I don't want to hear another squeak out of anyone!' BUT…
Lambs:	Baa, baa!
All:	Who's there now?
Leader:	Why, it's two little lambs with their shepherds. They are looking for the baby Jesus. And they know just where to find him… for the angels told them!
Angels:	Praise God in heaven! Peace on earth to everyone!

Sing the song 'O come, little children'
(*Carol, gaily carol*)

THE END

paste

paste

Knock, knock! Who's there?

It's baby Jesus

EPIPHANY: WHAT SHALL I GIVE?

Introduction

In this session, the children think about what makes a 'precious gift' (including presents that might be suitable for a baby) before they hear the story of the three wise men.

Ready...

Pack the story basket with some 'presents' that Teddy might consider giving his baby brother, only one of which is suitable for a baby—for example, a football, a toy car, a packet of sweets, a jigsaw and a game, with a suitable one such as a rattle, a mobile or a soft toy. Pack teddies to be Little Ted and Mrs Bear.

Steady...

Read Matthew 2; 1 Timothy 6:17–19

Go...

You're ready to encourage the children to take a delight in giving and to show that the most precious gifts are not always the most valuable. It's the thought that counts!

Let's begin!

Welcome

Welcome everyone! Especially…

For the adults

Although the festival of Epiphany originated in the east as a celebration of Christ's baptism, the Christian festival on 6 January celebrates the manifestation of Christ to the magi. Their gifts are appropriate for one who is 'king and God and sacrifice' (as in 'We three kings'). The most precious gifts we can give to children cannot be wrapped—our time, encouragement, enthusiasm, inspiration and praise.

Notices

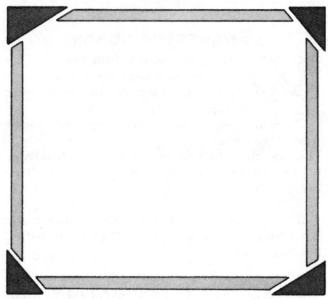

Sing Happy Birthday to...

The story basket

Remind the children that Teddy has a baby brother, and bring out Little Ted. Tell everyone that Teddy loves his brother very much and wants to buy him a present with the rest of his Christmas money. Isn't that kind of Teddy? Mrs Bear takes Teddy to the shops. He has a good look round. What can he find for little Ted? 'I'm sure Little Ted would like this,' says Teddy. What has he found? It's a great big black-and-white… football! Teddy bounces it on the floor. It's a wonderful ball. But Mrs Bear says that Little Ted's feet aren't strong enough to kick a ball yet, so Teddy puts it back where he found it.

Repeat with the other 'presents', explaining in each case why the present wouldn't be suitable. End with Teddy's delight in finding a suitable gift and giving it to Little Ted. In fact, it keeps the baby happy for such a long time that Mrs Bear has time to read Teddy an extra-long story!

(You could explain that babies grow up quite quickly and that, one day, Teddy will be able to play all sorts of games with his brother.)

> **God wants us to be loving and giving to other people.**

Suggested songs

Twinkle, twinkle little star
The north wind doth blow
What shall I give to the child in the manger? (*Carol, gaily carol*)
Some wise men in their splendour (*Carol, gaily carol*)
The first day of Christmas (*Carol, gaily carol*)
In the bleak midwinter (especially the last verse).

You may wish also to show the picture book *Give him my heart* by Debi Gliori, published by Bloomsbury.

Play acting

Ask the children to show a special present and tell you why it is precious to them. Perhaps it is from someone special or from an exotic place. Perhaps it was handmade by the giver, or very carefully chosen. Was it a surprise or was it something they had asked for? Begin with an example of your own.

Let the children take turns at being one of the wise men following the star to Joseph and Mary (with a baby doll) as everyone sings (to the tune of 'Three blind mice'):

Three wise men, three wise men;
see how they ride, see how they ride.
They all ride after the shining star
that shows them where Mary and Jesus are.
Did ever you carry a present so far
as three wise men?

Wise men: We bring you gold, frankincense and myrrh.
Mary and Joseph: Thank you very much for your precious gifts.

Nature notes

Bring in some sprays of winter jasmine and some snowdrops if they are out yet. Can the children see any bulbs beginning to push up through the soil to show that spring is on its way? Now that berries are scarce, the children could make bird-table food 'presents' for the birds as well as making sure that they have fresh water. Can the children see the difference between the blackbirds and the starlings? (Starlings are slightly smaller, they waddle instead of hopping, and their coats in winter are spotted and streaked with creamy white.) Put a compass on the nature table and let the children see in which direction the sun rises and sets. Go for a walk to find a weathervane. Open a book showing stars and comets.

Craft

Make card bookmarks in the shape of stars and comets for the children to decorate (see template, page 96). They can use the book-marks to point to where they are in their reading books or as gifts. Help the children to plait three pieces of brightly coloured wool or ribbon for the comet tail, to remind them of the three wise men following the star.

Decorate the star picture on page 95 and make a big comet to show in the story 'What can I give?'

Prayer

Ask _____ to read today's prayer.

Dear God, you have given us so many good things. What shall we give today? Perhaps we could give someone a helping hand or we could give some food to the hungry birds. Perhaps we could give someone a friendly smile. Thank you that it is such fun to give! Amen

What can I give?

I wonder if you have ever looked up into the sky at night and seen all the stars sparkling and twinkling? Perhaps they are the same stars that shone down on three wise men who lived when Jesus was born. In those days, there were no street lamps or electric lights in the cities, so the stars seemed extra bright. They glowed red and orange and green and blue—all the colours of the rainbow! *(Children hold up coloured star pictures from page 95.)*

The wise men loved to gaze at these stars. They knew all the patterns that they made in the darkness. So one night, the wise men were surprised to see a new star shining in the sky. *(Children hold up a sparkly comet.)*

'Look! Look over there, in the east!' cried Caspar, pointing his finger. 'There's a brilliant new star with a bright, shining head and a glittering tail!'

'Why, it's the most magnificent star I have ever seen!' gasped Melchior. 'Whatever can this mean?'

The wise men thought for a moment and suddenly they all knew the answer.

'Of course! The star is telling us that a new king has been born!' said Balthazar. 'And if that is his star, then he must be a most magnificent king—the King of kings, I should say!'

The three wise men wanted to visit the baby king. So they put saddles on their camels and packed the saddlebags with food and drink, ready for a long journey.

'I'm going to pack a present for the baby,' said Caspar. 'It would be very rude not to give him anything. Now what can I give?' Ummm!

'What can *I* give?' asked Melchior. Ummm!

'And what can *I* give?' asked Balthazar. Ummm!

They thought about many gifts that would be just right for a baby.

A woolly blanket, perhaps…? *(Hold up these gifts.)* Or a jar of honey…? A baby basket…?

But none of these seemed quite right.

'This baby is rather special,' said Caspar. 'So the presents we give him should be special too. Yes! I think I know what I'm going to take.'

'So do I,' said Melchior, smiling.

'And so do I,' said Balthazar, nodding wisely.

The three wise men packed their special gifts and rode on their camels for many days to the great city of Jerusalem.

'Where is the baby king?' they asked at the palace. 'We saw his star rise up in the east and we have come to kneel before him.'

King Herod frowned when he heard about a new king.

'*I* am the king,' he thought. 'We don't need another one!'

But he told the wise men where they would find the baby—in the town of Bethlehem.

'Do come back and tell me where his house is!' he told them, smiling rather too brightly. 'Then I will be able to take him a present too!'

The wise men rode towards Bethlehem.

'Look! There's the magnificent star again,' exclaimed Caspar.

'It's moving through the sky,' cried Melchior. 'It's just as if the star is leading us to the baby.'

'And look! It has stopped right over the town of Bethlehem,' said Balthazar. 'We will see the baby king very soon.'

He was quite right. The three wise men went into a house where they found baby Jesus with his mother Mary. They knelt down before the little king and presented him with their gifts.

'I have brought you gold because you are the King of kings,' said Caspar.

'I have brought you frankincense because you are the Son of God,' said Melchior. 'The sweet smell of frankincense reminds me of the temple where I worship God.'

'I have brought you a sweet-smelling spice called myrrh,' said Balthazar. 'We use it when we bury people who have died. I know it seems like a strange present for a baby, but it reminds me that you have come into the world to live and die, just like us!'

When they had finished admiring the baby, the three wise men went back home along a different road. They didn't want to tell King Herod where Jesus was because they were afraid he might try to harm the baby. I think that was very wise, don't you? What would *you* have given baby Jesus?

A star chart for home or school

deserves a star for:	Monday	Tuesday	Wednesday	Thursday	Friday		
smiling							
helping hands							
saying 'please' and 'thank you'							
sharing							
You choose!							

CANDLEMAS: LOOK AT OUR FAMILY!

Introduction

In this session, have fun involving the children in the baptism of Teddy's baby brother, Little Ted, before you tell them the story of Mary and Joseph presenting baby Jesus at the temple. You may like to invite your minister to pretend to baptize Little Ted.

Ready...

Pack the story basket with:
- various teddies of different sizes, including Mr and Mrs Bear and Little Ted
- a baby's christening robe or white nightdress
- a bowl (to represent the font)
- some water in a jug
- a candle and matches

Steady...

Read Luke 2:21–38; Ephesians 1:3–14

Go...

You're ready to use the idea of belonging to a family to help you explain that we all belong to God's wider family.

★ ★ ★

Let's begin!

Welcome

Welcome everyone! Especially…

For the adults

Candlemas on 2 February commemorates the presentation of Christ in the temple. This may be a good opportunity to encourage parents to think about baptizing their child so that he or she can make an informed decision about their faith in later years. For those who have already done so, or for any godparents, remind them that it is up to us to pray for the children in our care and to lead by example in taking part in the life and worship of the church.

Notices

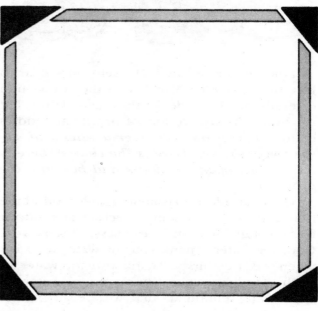

Sing Happy Birthday to...

....
....
....

The story basket

 Remind the children that Teddy belongs to a family and that he has a baby brother. *(Bring out Mr and Mrs Bear and Little Ted.)* Explain that when Little Ted was born, Teddy's grannies, grandpas, aunts and uncles came to see him and brought him presents to welcome him into the Bear family. But today, Little Ted is going to be baptized. That means he is going to be welcomed by all the people at his church into the church family.

Teddy is very excited. He helps Mrs Bear to give the baby a bath and then they dress him carefully. At 10 o'clock, they take Little Ted to church. There are lots of people at Teddy's church. *(Bring out the other teddies and say the finger-rhyme, 'Here is the church, here is the steeple, open the doors and here are the people'.)*

The vicar asks everyone to gather around the font and he pours some special water into it from a jug. Then the vicar says, 'Thank you, God, for water. Thank you for water to drink when we are thirsty. Thank you for water to wash in to keep clean. Thank you for water for baptism to remind us that we are all part of your family.' The vicar takes Little Ted in his arms and sprinkles some water over Little Ted's head. Then he makes the shape of a cross with his finger on Little Ted's forehead. *(Ask everyone to draw a cross shape in the air.)* Everyone in the church gives Little Ted a big clap to welcome him into the church family. *(All clap.)*

Just before they go home, Teddy is given a lighted candle to hold for his baby brother. It reminds Teddy of Jesus, who is the light of the world. Everyone in the church says, 'Shine like a star in the world, Little Ted, to show that you belong to God's family!' Afterwards, there is a wonderful party at the Bears' house and Teddy eats a big piece of the christening cake.

> **'Shine like a star in the world, Little Ted, to show that you belong to God's family!'**

Suggested songs

Pat-a-cake, pat-a-cake, baker's man
The farmer's in his den
Candle time *(Feeling Good!)*
You are welcome *(Feeling Good!)*
People we love *(Feeling Good!)*
The three bears *(Okki-tokki-unga)*
He's got the whole wide world *(Junior Praise)*
One more step along the world I go *(Junior Praise)*
Have you seen the pussy cat? *(Junior Praise)*

Play acting

Encourage the children to think about 'belonging' to something by asking them to bring in an object such as an item of club uniform, a school scarf or badge, ballet shoes or a family photograph. What do they do in their clubs or other groups? Talk about family likenesses.

Show them a cross necklace or a car sticker in the shape of a fish, worn or displayed as a sign of belonging to the Christian family.

Have a christening party for Little Ted and help the children to set the table for the Bear family, remembering to put out a baby's bowl, spoon and fork, plates, napkins and name cards. Everyone could dress up as aunts, uncles and cousins and pose with the Bears for a family photograph.

Nature notes

On the theme 'From darkness into light', talk about creatures that are waking up from their hibernation—hedgehogs, badgers, bats, ladybirds and snails peeping out of their shells. There is an old legend that the animals wake up on Candlemas day to see if the weather is mild enough for them to emerge yet.

Put some twigs in water and watch the buds opening up: children love hazel tree catkins that turn into fluffy yellow lamb's tails. Bring in a big book of plants or animals to show how they too belong to a family (for example, snowdrops are part of the daffodil family/our pet cats are related to lions and tigers). Can the children spot the similarities?

Craft

Show the children a postcard or print of the famous *Snail* painting by Matisse, *One of the Family* by F.G. Cotman or any formal family portrait from a stately home.

Make a christening card for Little Ted from the picture on page 94. The children could stick pictures of people, cut from magazines, around the family shown. Then fold the sides into the middle to hide the picture and make the two flaps into church doors by adding round doorknob stickers.

You could help the children to make their own family tree using photographs brought from home.

Prayer

Ask _____ to read today's prayer.

Dear Father God, thank you that we are all your children. Thank you for letting us belong to your big family. Please help us to make the world a bright place by looking after one another, as brothers and sisters should. Amen

Look at our family!

When baby Jesus was just a few weeks old, Mary and Joseph took him to the temple, the place where people worshipped God. They felt very happy and proud. Before Jesus was born, there were just the two of them. But now there were three. As they walked along, everyone smiled at Mary as if to say, 'Congratulations on your new baby!'

Inside the temple sat an old man with a kind face. His name was Simeon. Simeon was watching all the people coming into the building. It was just as if he was waiting for someone. As soon as he saw the baby in Mary's arms, his face lit up. His eyes twinkled and a big smile spread across his face. 'Why, this is the special child that God told me about,' he thought. 'God promised me that I would see him.'

Mary let Simeon hold her baby. The old man held out his little finger and the baby grasped it in his tiny hand. At this, Simeon chuckled.

'Oh, thank you, God, for letting me see this baby just as you promised,' he said, with shining eyes. 'This baby lights up my life, and when he grows up, he will light up the world. God bless you, Mary and Joseph. God bless your new family.'

As you can imagine, Mary and Joseph were amazed at the things that Simeon said. How did he know that Jesus was such a special baby? But before they could ask him, an old lady called Anna saw the baby too.

'Thank you, God, for this wonderful child!' she cried, just as Simeon had done. 'This is the child we have been waiting for,' she explained to everyone in the temple.

On the way home, Mary and Joseph thought about all the people they had met because of their new baby—shepherds from the hillside, three wise men and now Simeon and Anna. Somehow, they all knew that Jesus was no ordinary child.

Whatever was going to happen next?

A christening card for you to make

Welcome to the church family

With love from

Star template for sessions 9 and 11

Comet template for session 11

Star and comet template for bookmark in session 11